Where Are My "Jesus I Can Do Anything" Socks?

By Edna Blake

First Printing, November 1998

For information contact Edna Blake at :
14 Merribrook Court • O'Fallon, MO • 63366

ISBN: 0-9668906-0-4

Scripture Quotations, used by permission are from:
The Touchpoint Bible - The New Living Translation 1996

Cover and illustrations by Kathy Allen, St. Louis, MO

Printed in the United States of America.

This book is dedicated to:
Bill, who taught me about alliteration and **completing** the task. He was **called** home much too soon.
Dan, who **continued** to **call**, asking, "Have you started the book?"
Tim, who **corrected** my **copy** and made me look **cool**.
Mike, who **considered** what I had written and **commented**, "Mom, this is **challenging**."

Table of Contents

Introduction 6

Chapter One   Come As You Are! 9

Chapter Two   Circles of Change 21

Chapter Three Confronted With Grace 39

Chapter Four   Caring Communication 53

Chapter Five   Calm Verses The Storm 73

Chapter Six   Come On Down! 89

Chapter Seven Courting Deception 107

Chapter Eight Camping Out 123

Chapter Nine   Count Your Blessings 137

Chapter Ten   Carry On! .157

Introduction

People write books from all walks of life. Each of us could probably write several books. We write because we have experienced life. Some of us journal as a form of writing to keep track of details and happenings in our lives. This book is about some of the events in my life and of my family. It takes a great deal of courage to write a book like this because it lays open personal things. It also takes endurance to wait for the book to be published.

I wanted to write this book to share about my relationship with God; in particular, how it is an on-going **process**. I hope you will be encouraged as you read this book. It may help you think about your own process with God. Hopefully, as the thoughts are shared, you will find yourself laughing and crying....maybe on the same page.

Someone told me that the word for the 90's was "**PROCESS**". People's careers and their relationships are all part of a process today. I believe this book is about the **process** of life, and living it out as we discover who we are "In Christ". I recall teaching a Sunday School class in 'Tropical' Minnesota. We studied the book of Ephesians. During that time I realized again the importance of knowing who we are "In Christ." I was impressed with how knowing who we are "In Christ" really defined the **process** for me.

I read somewhere that the introduction of any book should be for the purpose of giving the reader information on why you wrote the book in order to whet their appetite to read beyond the introduction. The concept sounded pretty good until I began to ask people how many of them read the introduction first. Very few people read the introduction. So then I thought it might be really important to have a classy cover that will entice the reader to get into the book. I then learned that many skim to the middle of the book and toward the end. Well, so much for my knowledge of book marketing. I'm not even sure if they look at the cover or the first chapter! And since this is only the introduction, I'm just glad you're here!

I do know many of my readers are my friends and know my family. And many are from the family of people who have followed my ministry efforts in conferences and Bible studies and radio broadcasts in Minnesota. I am pleased that you have been able to share in this part of my life, my writing. You may be in the middle of your own process and are interested in how God used my process to refine and define me as a Christian. In any case, I trust you will be encouraged in your relationship with God as you read this book.

Oh yes, thanks to my family for allowing me to share our family stuff, and to my many friends who believed in me. But mostly, I thank God for using someone like me to encourage and disciple His people.

Chapter One

COME AS YOU ARE

As a child and as a woman I wanted to be accepted. I wanted to be accepted by my friends. Later, I wanted a very special someone to accept me, someone that would get to know me and still be open to accepting me as I was. It is important to have that acceptance in our lives. Acceptance from others helps us to develop our personalities and our own self worth.

It can be difficult to grasp the importance of accepting ourselves as the person God made us to be. This slow process offers hidden obstacles because, as you know, we begin by comparing ourselves with one another. This kind of thinking is very common and very unproductive. We have to get beyond the negative thinking that we must be like someone else or live up to their expectations in order to be accepted. In the Christian world, as we are searching for support and acceptance, we naturally wonder if God accepts us. It is transitional thinking, process thinking, that brings us to the important question. We eventually question our personal worth based upon whether or not we believe God has accepted us. I finally concluded that indeed God must love and accept me based upon what he reveals to us in the Bible.

This was a major breakthrough for me. Having this knowledge in my heart truly affected my whole life and the course of events which have come my way by the hand of God. God is constantly drawing us closer to himself. A first step in acknowledging God working in our lives is seeing him draw us closer to him. It is the process of walking in step with the Spirit.

Do you remember those crazy parties called "Come as you are" parties? Your friends would come to your house, pick you up at some ungodly hour, take you off to the designated party place. Your hair would be a mess, your teeth not brushed. Of course, you would leave looking your all-time best. Ha! At the party our so-called friends would appear laughing, joking, and drag us off to yet another friend's place. And that was supposed to cheer us up and make us feel loved and cared about. We were supposed to be having FUN!

So many of us look at our lives and feel like we have been invited to a party. And we have "come as we are", but only to discover we haven't been invited. And the invitation we received has someone else's name on it. Naturally, we feel lost and out of place. There is no name tag for us. This is not a good confidence builder.

We all have learned to pretend...to perform...to adjust...to blend into our society, church, and family. We may look as though we are well adjusted, happy, full of life and energy, but without a clue as to who we are and what we are about as a person.

When you and I **come as we are**, into his kingdom, we do not have to be concerned about who we are and how we fit into this new life In Christ. Our identity is in Christ. It takes some time to adjust and understand how this affects our personal lives, our philosophy. It is a growing process. God has accepted us and he has a plan for our lives, a plan for success and a plan that will bring us into a deeper relationship with him. He desires to affirm us in who we are.

For years I was known as Bill Blake's wife. Then he died and I was just Edna Blake. It was essential for me to remember that am acceptable as an individual, and my identity is and always will be who I am In Christ. Identity, and clarification of who we are, comes when we discover and understand **who we are in Christ**. Such a simple statement, but what does it have to do with anything when we are struggling with acceptance and personal meaning for our lives?

In circumstances like this, unhealthy thinking from our past comes clearly into focus. We find that we cannot totally erase this negative thinking and its influence upon our lives. We search for years hoping to discover our purpose and what it means to be truly accepted by the Lord and others. This search for acceptance can be an overwhelming process. And we just want it to be done with and our lives settled.

God in his grace allows us the time to discover his character while at the same time teaching us who we really are. But when we spend time focusing on ourselves rather than focusing on God our chances of getting a grip on the truth can get shelved. We tend to get into all sorts of unhealthy ways of coping when we are not at peace with who we are in Christ.

Feeling Accepted = Someone must love me! Could it be God?

We must recognize that God is the source of wisdom. He alone knows the questions and the answers. The thread of untruth runs through our sick sifters, and we actually believe that in some way God doesn't care or want us. We imagine this rejection. It does not come from God. Our distorted view of God produces distorted thinking. We allow our thinking to assimilate the secular values of this world. We forget that God's truth transcends time and is above all other understanding. He is the one who made us, knows all about us, and wants to reveal Himself to us. He wants to guide us through our process until we know for certain that we are loved and accepted by Him. The lies should have no control over us. When we ask for wisdom, He will give it to us. Whatever we need, He will Provide.

When the Prodigal Son came to the end of himself he faced the fact that his only choice was to go back home, hoping that his father would still accept him. He did not know for certain if his father would accept him or not. He needed to hear the words of acceptance from his father's lips. (Luke 15:11-32). The father loved his son because they had a relationship. He just loved him and accepted him because he was his son. He did not necessarily approve of his choices but he loved him unconditionally.

Some of you cannot relate to the love of an earthly father in this way, but our Heavenly Father does accept and love us *unconditionally*. We get fooled into thinking we must always be perfect, do the right things in order to be accepted by the

14

heavenly Father. The only thing we can **do** is to accept the provision of what Jesus **did** on the cross for our sins. Jesus paid for our sins and our relationship with God is based upon what Christ **did** on the cross. When we understand this concept for our lives it changes how we feel about the pressure of needing to be accepted by others.

Peer pressure is still very real today. Who doesn't want to feel as though they have a special place where they belong? We all get caught in the trap of so wanting a place to feel needed and accepted. We get distracted and our focus becomes fuzzy. Sometimes this is because of the stress in our lives. We might feel that God is off on a vacation, or that He has moved and left no forwarding address. I have been there too. I pray that God will again reveal Himself to you through sending someone to remind you of His great love and concern for you.

Our thinking process needs a spiritual revision. Understanding *who we are in Christ* includes several very basic concepts. As we come to understand them more clearly we will actually start walking in the Spirit. It is so freeing.

Walking in the Spirit:

> 1. The same power that raised Jesus from the dead, the Holy Spirit is now alive and working in us. We are in this world, but we do not have to participate in this world. We have a new nature. We are one with Christ and with all other believers. We are part of the body of Christ.

> 2. We were at one time far away from God, but now we are part of His family because of the death

of Christ upon the cross. The blood of Christ was shed for our sins. He died as a substitute for our sins. He paid the price for our sins and satisfied the justice of God.

3. The hostility that once kept us apart now draws us together. There is neither Jew, Gentile, slave or free, male or female. We are one in Christ.

I remember how thrilled Bill and I were when we were accepted by Inter-Varsity to join their staff team. We were going to be joining a staff team that would be working directly with college students. We enthusiastically believed that college students were the hope of our future. We would be helping them to come to know Christ in a personal way. We would be modeling and discipling students. *A high calling in our minds.*

We had survived the application forms, the interviews. As we were in our forties then, we had been informed that we were accepted as the oldest new staff on the Inter-Varsity staff team, (IVCF STAFF TEAM). Everything was communicated to us in bold capital acronyms, official looking buzz phrases. You would see them in every piece of communication coming from the main office. It wouldn't have surprised me to see us referred to as OLD STAFF.

We were thrilled to find ourselves at the training camp for NEW STAFF. My job assignment, along with two other great gals, was cleaning the bathrooms. It all seemed so laughable because serving God and being called to train students in Discipleship, Evangelism and Missions didn't seem to have anything to do with cleaning toilets...Imagine my surprise when I discovered that it had everything to do with serving students. Our calling was to serve God, and to serve students. Leadership is all about servanthood. It will always be about doing whatever is required. If we say we want to lead we must be willing to serve. If we just keep waiting for the really big and important places of leadership to come our way we will be discontent and we will find it difficult to serve God.

This was: "Toilet Training Discipline 101"

We were gathered together in this large room, as NEW STAFF. We were in a circle facing one another. There were perhaps ten couples and several single people coming on STAFF at this time. We were all equally excited with the potential prospects of serving students at our assigned campuses. The NEW STAFF, along with the seasoned staff people were there, including Dr. Alexander, the president of the organization. It was a very big deal. I was so green... I didn't know enough to be really impressed, or scared. I was just excited.

All of them were well educated. They knew all about Missions, Discipleship and Evangelism. They had read and had total understanding of the "great staff manual." Some of them had written the staff manuals. We were there to be motivated and trained to serve on our assigned campuses.

We were asked to go around the circle and give our names and share a little about ourselves. I thought that request a bit simplistic since we all had name tags. No doubt it was just a reality check to see if we could still tell who we were.

"I'm....so and so, and this is my wife...so and so," and the husband would give his wife's name, continuing on... "and we have attended this or that college, and our degrees are in Education or English"... on and on around the room. The single staff said who they were and what degrees they had. It was a great group of men and women. These folks were by any man's standard the cream of the crop. I was impressed.

They came from the cities and from the plains...all across the United States. Everyone seemed to be very well put together...it was all so proper and so formal. I thought "How does all of this relate to ministering with students?"

It was finally our turn. We had almost gone completely around the circle, and Bill said, "Hello, I'm Bill", and he mentioned his degrees and the schools he had attended, and then he turned to me. I said, "I'm Edna, **I am here because I am too ugly to kiss good-bye**." They needed some comic relief. It was getting much too serious. We all laughed.

To me it didn't really matter how we got there or who we were because God had accepted us In Christ to serve together in that place. **Having a calling and coming as you are** makes all the difference in the world. God does not call us based upon what we know, who we are, where we have been, how many degrees we have or don't have. He calls us based upon **who we are in Christ**.

He calls us, and equips us to be whatever he needs us to be. He knows what will be required and he has given us the gifts we need to complete the task. Some are evangelists and some are teachers, and some are encouragers...all are needed in the ministry of serving students.

When **we come as we are**, we must depend upon Him and His Holy Spirit. Without Him...we can do nothing. Who we are, what we have done, what we know... really doesn't matter if we aren't sure of who we are "In Christ". This priority thinking will carry us through the process of serving God. It establishes who is responsible and who is in charge. We

wrestle with this authority question again and again through-
out our time of being Christians. Sometimes the way we were
and the way it was isn't a good picture.

Ephesians 1:3-14

"Praise be to the God and Father of our Lord
Jesus Christ, who has blessed us in the heavenly
realms with every spiritual blessing in Christ. For
he chose us in him before the creation of the world
to be holy and blameless in his sight. In love he
predestined us to be adopted as sons through Jesus
Christ in accordance with his pleasure and will to the
praise of his glorious grace, which he has freely given
us in the One he loves. In him we have redemption
through his blood, the forgiveness of sins, in
accordance with the riches of God's grace that he
lavished on us with all wisdom and understanding.
And he made known to us the mystery of his will
according to his good pleasure, which he purposed
in Christ, to be put into effect when the times will
have reached their fulfillment—to bring all things
in heaven and on earth together under one head,
even Christ.

In Him we were also chosen, having been predestined
according to the plan of him who works out
everything in conformity with the purpose of his
will, in order that we, who were the first to hope in
Christ, might be for the praise of his glory. And you
also were included in Christ when you heard the
word of truth, the gospel of your salvation. Having
believed, you were marked in him with a seal, the
promised Holy Spirit, who is a deposit guaranteeing
our inheritance until the redemption of those who
are God's possession—to the praise of his glory." *NLT*

19

We can come as we are...anytime, anyplace, anywhere...if we have accepted this call upon our lives. We have the seal of the Holy Spirit upon us. We can come as we are knowing that God will be with us in whatever we are attempting to be or do. When we know this truth we will not tend to rely upon our feelings for affirmation. Often feelings have come through our sick sifter, and what we perceive from our feelings is not true at all.

When we know Him we grow in our understanding of what it means to be *In Christ*. It is important to not rely upon our feelings. He is faithful to His Word. What He says He will do. He will provide the strength we need to be and do whatever He calls us to do. *We are in Christ and He enables us to do what He is calling us to do.*

Walking in step with the Spirit doesn't mean that our lives won't have problems. It doesn't mean that at times we will not make poor choices. We do have to live with the results of those poor choices. It doesn't mean that we will not be hurt by the disobedience of others, and at times our own disobedience, but it does mean that we have a resource. He will be there! He is never late or slow. His timing is impeccable.

> **Habakkuk 2:3**
> "If it seems slow, wait patiently, for it will surely take place. It will not be delayed." *NLT*

He is my help in times of trouble. He is my fortress when I need a place to hide. He is my Shepherd when I feel like a lost sheep. **He is the Main Thing**...and we must remember that the main thing is knowing Him. When we **come as we are**, we will be accepted by the One who really matters.

Consider This:

1. How does self-esteem and knowing who you are "in Christ" relate to your daily life?

2. If our self-confidence is not in balance with the Word we will constantly be feeling that we have no value and no worth. Do you find it hard to view yourself from God's perspective?

Pride and false humility will rob us of the joy of being content and at peace with who we are. We will be ruled by fear and afraid to **come as we are**.

_____

_____

_____

_____

_____

Chapter Two

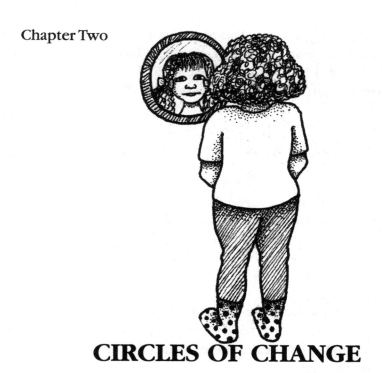

CIRCLES OF CHANGE

"What do you do when company's coming...and the oven breaks down...the dog throws up on the rug...your husband calls and says he's running a little late and can't pick up the cheese for the lasagna which you need before you can put it in the oven which for some reason doesn't seem to be working just now...?" **Be Flexible!**

Have you ever thought that if you actually do make it through the day you'll surely be raptured and your life will be over? Some of the days of our lives are real life epic adventures. We all are faced with **the fact of being caught up with change**. Change can be good and it can be challenging. It doesn't necessarily have to be a negative experience for us; however to learn that in the midst of change we are called to be flexible. This then is process.

Every day is an opportunity to see God and His mercy being demonstrated toward us. But we say, "This is not what I signed up for. I know this is not what I signed up for". **Flexibility**, isn't that one of the fruits of the Spirit?

Love, joy, peace, Patience, kindness, goodness, faithfulness, gentleness and self-control......

I didn't see **flexibility** in the midst of that verse from Galatians 5:20. But we do need to be **flexible** if we are to survive and have the fruits of the Spirit working in our lives. God calls us to perseverance while we are living our lives, which seems to address the idea of **constant change**. This is process.

James 1:2-8
"Consider it pure joy, by brothers, and sisters, whenever you face trials of many kinds, because you know that the testing of your faith develops perseverance." *NLT*

CHANGE HAPPENS!

Don't change...stay the way you are. This is a wonderful sounding concept, but all of us need to change.

James 1: 17
"Don't be deceived, my dear brothers. Every good and perfect gift is from above, coming down from the Father of the heavenly lights, who does not change like shifting shadows." *NLT*

We know that we all change, but God never changes.

My mother used to forever be moving the furniture around in our house. My father was a shift worker. He came home late in the night. His usual habit was to leave the bathroom light on, go into the bedroom sit down on his bed, take off his shoes and get ready for bed. His bed on this particular night was not there. He was sitting in the middle of the floor.

My mother had moved the furniture again and moved his bed. They had twin beds. This was the 1940's. My dad had all he could deal with...this was the final move for him. It was two in the morning, and he began hammering nails in the legs of the bed. He was nailing his bed to the floor. She could still move all the furniture in the house, but she was not going to be able to move his bed. You could say this was the last nail. He didn't say a word.

I laugh when I remember this event in the lives of my parents. Change can be a good thing, but sometimes because we are so busy, we just want the comfort of the familiar. I am grateful that God doesn't change. He is the same today, tomorrow, and forever.

About the time I manage to settle in on a routine, or think I have figured out the moves, it changes. Bill, my husband, thrived on change. I used to think, "Why can't our lives be just a little bit more like everyone else's?" I was looking for normal in all the wrong places. From the time we are born we are changing and we are dying every day. It is a little hard for me to accept, but I know it is true. The seasons are designed by God to remind us that our lives have similar patterns.

Ecclesiates 3:1-14
"There is a time for everything,
    a season for every activity under heaven.
A time to be born and a time to die.
    A time to plant and a time to harvest.

A time to kill and a time to heal.
A time to tear down and a time to rebuild.
A time to cry and a time to laugh.
A time to grieve and a time to dance.
A time to scatter stones and a time to gather stones.
A time to embrace and a time to turn away.
A time to search and a time to lose.
A time to keep and a time to throw away.
A time to tear and a time to mend.
A time to be quiet and a time to speak up.
A time to love and a time to hate.
A time for war and a time for peace." *NLT*

"What do people really get for all their hard work? I have thought about this in connection with the various kinds of work God has given people to do. God has made everything beautiful for its own time. He has planted eternity in the human heart, but even so, people cannot see the whole scope of God's work from beginning to end. So I concluded that there is nothing better for people than to be happy and to enjoy themselves as long as they can. And people should eat and drink and enjoy the fruits of their labor, for these are gifts from God. And I know that whatever God does is final. Nothing can be added to it or taken from it. God's purpose is this, that people should fear Him. Whatever exists today and whatever will exist in the future has already existed in the past. For God calls each event back in its turn." *NLT*

Change is inevitable!

People can choose to participate with God's plan and see His purpose in it...or people can rebel, and we will still see His plan and purpose. God works in my life in spite of me. **He**

supports and loves me, because no plan of His will be thwarted and His purpose will be perfected in my life. It seems to make me happier if I participate willingly, but it isn't always the way I choose to respond to God's working in my life.

The changes haven't always suited me because I didn't feel God gave me enough notice. Sometimes I don't respond in an appropriate way. I don't want to just accept it when I don't feel prepared. My actions can display my need to be a control freak. But this is not always Godly either.

> **Philippians. 1:6**
> "And I am sure that God, who began the good work within you, will continue his work until it is finally finished on that day when Christ Jesus comes back again." *NLT*

I see **change** in my children...Tim is losing his sense of smell, Dan his hearing, and Mike his hair. Those **changes** are there for us to observe. I am getting gray, slower in my step, forgetful, and not as agile as I used to be...all part of God's plan for our lives. There is a natural flow for each of us. It is the aging process. Each of us must face the fact that our days have been numbered by the Lord. Physically we change. Emotionally we change. Spiritually we are changing. God is aware of the whole person because He is the Creator God. He made each of us special and unique. He knows everything there is to know about us. We can trust God with every aspect of who we are, and in the midst of change He will still be there. We know this intellectually, but often we have not transferred what we know into walking it out in faith. Our confidence is not in what we know, but in Whom we know.

If we are known by Him, then there should be nothing that

concerns us. True, until we come to the place where we must face change or be called upon to face the by-product of change which is **transition**. This transitional step is happening at the same time we are moving forward to the next stage of living our lives. When we don't know the plan it can be very scary. It would be great if we could all embrace this next step as just the way it is, but we aren't always walking in the Spirit and we aren't always relying on the Holy Spirit to give us courage to change. The strongest of us can become fearful and full of doubt.

I used to sing a little song to myself. It said: "Don't be afraid, don't be afraid, Jesus will help you, so don't be afraid." I taught this little song to my children. This didn't mean that at times I wasn't scared or that bad things didn't happen. It just meant that in the midst of it I would try to remember that my resource was the Holy Spirit. Jesus promised that He would be with me and that He would guide me throughout the next step. It is often clearly an experience of His discipline, and not just pure happenstance. I have to rely upon Him, and He promises to be there. God uses His promises to encourage us. He is faithful to His promises.

He is the God of Transitions!

I moved again. This was my 29th move since I married Bill. Moving was what he considered to be normal. I was continuing in this tradition. I had decided to take early retirement and move back to the St. Louis area where I could be close to my sons and their families. I also moved my Mom back from Minnesota to Missouri. When we arrived at my new home, it was late in the afternoon. A hot humid typical summer day in St. Louis. July 7th, in all of its glory. It was a big change from living in Minnesota. It was 'Truly Tropical'. This would be an adjustment. We were exhausted. And then God did a wonderful thing. It just happened. God came to the rescue.

The little children in my new neighborhood asked if they could be of help in unloading all of my boxes. I had boxes and boxes. I had all this stuff that I brought with me from Minnesota. Stuff that I called antiques. Some of the boxes were full of my husband's books. I could not part with them.

Jason, Jenny, Joshua, Andrea, Chris, Brenda and Michael... others too, but I didn't know their names. These children came to the rescue. All the stuff was piled to the ceiling of the garage. The children welcomed me to my new community.

"Unless you come as little children you cannot be accepted into His kingdom." Leave all the pretense and performance behind. The transition and the change meant I was now going to live in a new place, and the change had to do with God's plan and purpose, not mine.

That night in my old bed but new bedroom I tried to sleep. The familiar sounds of the train and the smells of the paper mill were 740 miles away. I had moved from the last place where Bill and I had lived together. This time I had moved without Bill. The new sound of a dog barking in the distance was the last thing I heard before I fell to sleep in peace. The challenge of changes can be seen in these thoughts.

- Many changes are uncharted courses, something we've never done, and this can be intimidating.
- We may feel all alone and fearful in the process of this change.
- Our feelings may be insecurity, may threaten to disrupt an established working pattern. In this

way we may end up allowing our feelings to chart the course in a wrong direction.

- This change is may not be exactly what we had in mind. We feel forced into something undesirable, and now we are dealing with our anger along with the change.
- We may have sinned in our change and in the process lost our feeling of spiritual connection with God so we don't feel forgiven.

In any analysis, we have to always remember that no plan of God can be thwarted, as it says in Job 43:1-2. We need to always look for His hand in the change and embrace it before allowing our humanity to interfere.

My husband's health started failing shortly after our time with Inter-Varsity. We had worked for them in Minnesota for seven and one half years.

We moved back to St. Louis, where Bill took the position of an associate pastor. I was thrilled to be back in the area, close to friends and family. It was exciting to be in an area where I would not have to worry about snow, cold winters and plugging our cars in overnight so they would start in the sub-zero temperatures the next day. Another plus was a swimming pool in our back yard. It seemed like I had died and found myself in St. Louis, which seemed to me like heaven.

The church was an exciting place to be ministering. We were leading small groups in the church, and training people for positions of leadership. This happens to be one of my passions, and we were riding the crest of the wave, or so I thought. Isn't it just like our human nature to have a total different view of our lives apart from God's perspective. It is important to view ourselves and our lives through God's eyes and His plan. I occasionally need a spiritual reality check.

It seemed too good to be true, and then one day Bill came home from the office and simply stated, "We're moving back to Minnesota." I said, "No way. I'm not moving anywhere, much less back to Minnesota." I had just spent seven and one half years in Minnesota, and I absolutely didn't want to move back to the frozen tundra. I had been away from my grandchildren and our kids, and I wasn't going to do that again. His reply came back clear, and with even more determination, "I know that God has called me to go back to Minnesota. Health wise, I cannot live here. Everyday I feel like I am choking. I cannot breath." I know now he was struggling with the beginning stages of his severe health problems. He had asthma, diabetes and a heart condition.

I could not understand this decision. It seemed selfish to me. I didn't want any part of the move. He told me that he was moving and I could choose to come along or not. His frustration was apparent in that statement. We finally ended up going to a marriage counselor for three months. Bill made a covenant with me at the time...AND we did move.

This was the covenant:

> "Edna,
> As a preface to working on "what we have that is worth building on," let me first say this:
> 1. I agree that future major decisions will not be made without dual agreement in advance -e.g.. housing, transportation purchases, stewardship commitments, major budgeting allotments, ministry commitments, etc.
> 2. Specifically—no decision to relocate geographically or to re-focus occupationally will be made without mutual agreement and to agree that the time to

change has truly arrived: (if the change effects both of our ministries—that your ministry is ready for change as well as mine).

I hope that this will give you enough genuine hope to work together with me toward a true reconciliation of our marriage relationship so that it can become healthier and more mutually rewarding than it ever has been before.

I want us to both be healthy and happy with each other and jointly productive in the Lord's work wherever we are located geographically-I think it is fair to expect that some of our work will be together; some will be on an individual nature, but all will function in concert and in enthusiastic support of one another before God and man. I am willing to, and committed to, making personal changes which are mutually agreed upon as necessary in order to make this work.

Whenever it appears to you that I am not living up to or acting in the spirit of this statement please gently help me to see your point of view on the matter so that you and I can both feel good about making corrections in my behavior....
signed, "Bill" dated June 24, 1987

I share this personal insight of my life to allow you to see how important it was for me to know how I also wanted to be in control. I did not want to change or be changed and I cared very little about "God's will" at that point. I wanted to be and do what I wanted. I wanted to stay in St. Louis to live out my comfortable little life.

But God had a very unique plan for my life. It was God's plan to care for me in the next few years in a very special way. The move was really for my benefit. The changes were necessary so that when my dear husband passed away in May of 1993 I would be in a safe place. I would have a job. I would be where people could surround me and care for me and my Mom. I would be safe until such a time when I would be able to move back to St. Louis. It really was God's plan to care for me. But I fought this because I did not know what was best for me. We often do not know what is best for us. I am so glad that Bill could hear from God at this point of our lives.

God was looking out for me, I just didn't realize it.

Our need **for control is sometimes so strong we forget that God has the plan.** God cares and loves us, and He wants what is best for us. He knows today, tomorrow, and the future. Yes, He has promised to provide, but how do we come to understand that provision in our lives? Sometimes it is when we are removed from our comfort zone. When we have been stripped of our plans and the dead end, no growth thinking, then God starts the process of working in our lives in spite of our denial of the truth. **The move was for me**. It was God providing a safe place for me when He took Bill home to be with Him.

Change Develops our Character.

Joseph in the Bible is a prime example of a person who faced change. Let me tell his story to illustrate. It goes like this:

Joseph was the favored son of his father, Jacob. Because he knew he was the favored son, Joseph used this knowledge to lord it over his brothers. He even tried to lord it over his father, but his father wasn't having any of it. This behavior on

Joseph's part caused his brothers to become very angry with him. They decided to kill him. As a caravan was passing by on it's way to Egypt they determined to sell him into slavery instead.

This episode from his life took him out of his safe and secure environment completely. He was moved out of his safe place, put in a totally different culture. If he had any tendency toward arrogance he would be stripped of it by the school of hard knocks and by being forced to experience life as a slave. When the caravan arrived in Egypt Joseph found himself a slave to a man named Potiphar. Eventually Potiphar saw Joseph's great potential and placed him in a position of authority over his household. Joseph was a responsible person. Potiphar saw his stability and organizational skills. He gave Joseph the responsibility of being in charge of his household, second in command.

God then took him through another time of testing. Perhaps Potiphar failed to ask his wife if she thought it was a good idea to promote Joseph to this position. Maybe Potiphar's wife was not happy to have Joseph second in command, however the scenario went. She was also very attracted to him physically. Potiphar's wife made sexual advances toward Joseph. He resisted with his character intact.

Joseph was tested beyond what most of us ever have to encounter. But even as he passed the testing he was thrown into prison. He was history! It causes us to ask how a man whom God was going to use for a very responsible position could be put in such a dilemma.

It gets worse. While in prison, he proved to be so trustworthy that he was again placed in a responsible position. He is in prison and he is still experiencing God's favor. He was now made responsible for the prisoners. There are two other significant prisoners in the story. The baker and the king's cup bearer were thrown into prison as well. God had a plan, and the baker and the king's cup bearer were part of the plan. Time passed, and the baker and the cup bearer each had a dream. Joseph was able to tell them the interpretations of their dreams. God gave to Joseph the wisdom he needed to discern the meaning of the dreams for both the baker and the kings cup-bearer. The cup bearer returned to his position in the palace, but the baker was killed. Joseph asked the cup bearer to remember the kindness he had shown him, and to get him out of prison, but the cup bearer forgot about Joseph. This reads like your worst nightmare.

It must have seemed to Joseph that perhaps God had forgotten him. This was God's dress rehearsal for really testing his character and building him up for the next episode. It may have looked like Joseph was a loser but he was learning the lesson of his God being in control.

Two years later, the cup bearer finally remembered that Joseph could interpret dreams. Joseph faced major changes in his life. Some he could predict, but in others situations it seemed like he was waiting upon someone to remember him. **Changes are in our lives for the purpose of developing our character**.

GOD REMEMBERED AND WAS AWARE OF JOSEPH THE WHOLE TIME.

It had nothing to do with the cup bearer remembering. It was the timing of God. Joseph was released from prison to interpret a dream for the king, and Joseph did tell him the meaning of his dream. Joseph told the king about the famine that was coming and counseled him as to what he should do. The king believed everything Joseph told him and saw potential in him as a person. The king needed that wisdom if they were to survive the next 14 years. The king gave him a wife and placed him in a position of leadership. This **all happened to reveal God's plan to provide for the entire nation of Israel**. God has a plan...and change develops our character. We serve the purpose of God through the living out of our lives, and again it's about the *process*.

The famine happened just as Joseph said it would. His brothers came down to get help for themselves and their families. They came face to face with their past and their brother. But they did not know it was Joseph. He spoke to them through an interpreter and they only knew that this man had the key to their survival.

Finally after two visits to Egypt, they brought back their father and their younger brother. Joseph requested this of them in order to see his father and brother again. This story is a classic example of God once again taking His people through change in order to reveal His character to them and prove how He does care for them in the times of great difficulty. We see Joseph being refined by God in the book of Genesis.

Meanwhile, Joseph reveals himself to his brothers, and **Voila!** Immediately they think, *Now* he will really get us. But not so. We get a glimpse of God's purpose and plan as God defines mercy for us by this real life example. Terrible things happen to real people. God uses the circumstances to reveal his plan and his character.

As part of this story, I have found these verses in Genesis to be a source of hope and encouragement when I have felt overwhelmed and discouraged. I have been so tired of waiting for God to move. These verses gave me hope. I quote them here.

Genesis 45:4

"'Come over here,' he said, so they came closer. And he said again, 'I am Joseph, your brother whom you sold into Egypt. But don't be angry with yourselves that you did this to me, for God did it. He sent me here ahead of you to preserve your lives.'" *NLT*

Genesis 50:19-21

"But Joseph told them, 'Don't be afraid of me. Am I God, to judge and punish you? As far as I am concerned, God turned into good what you meant for evil. He brought me to the high position I have today so I could save the lives of many people. No, don't be afraid. Indeed, I myself will take care of you and your families.' And he spoke very kindly to them, reassuring them." *NLT*

Consider This:

1. Do I really want to be changed, for God to develop my character?
2. We need to admit to God that we are not always excited about change. We may pray to God to help us grow, but then when the change and circumstances occur it can challenge our ideas of what we think spiritual growth really means. Sometimes God takes us through complicated choices to force us to depend upon Him and not ourselves.
3. Is God working in your life through your present circumstances to bring you into a closer relationship with Him? Maybe it hasn't been viewed by you as a positive working of God in your life. Tell someone else your heart on this matter and ask them to pray with you. Ask God for the strength to carry on.
4. Are we ready to go anywhere, do anything, in order to serve God and His purpose?
5. Have I asked God to reveal His purpose to me, knowing that in the Circles of Change the main purpose is that He would be glorified?
6. Would I be willing to forgive like Joseph, who gladly for gave his brothers?

_____

_____

_____

_____

_____

Notes

Chapter Three

CONFRONTED WITH GRACE

I don't enjoy the kind of situations that cause me to wonder if I will even get through the day. I don't even pretend to understand what it means to get through my whole life. I can only handle one hour at a time, and a whole day takes a lot of prayer. Living in the present is becoming more of my style than it used to be.

Most people view me as this very out-going person. I am not. The concept of learning that I could **Come as I am** opened all sorts of doors for me. It started with cracks and then windows, but now I know that I am accepted by God and He is working through all of the changes. He actually wants to use me in the ministry of bringing others to Him and helping others to learn about His grace.

He accepts me and He wants you to learn this truth as well.

The Circles of Change in my life have convinced me that no matter what is happening, God will be there. The next phase of my **process** has to do with accepting the fact that God, the Creator, loves me and offers me **grace**. This truth has been revealed to me by the presence and activity of the Holy Spirit in my life. He gives me holy boldness. God is actively at work in my life on a daily basis.

The concepts I find in Scripture also become active and evident in my life. "He uses the weak things to confound the wise...and the foolish things of this world to minister and bless others." I see this as a very clear indication for any of us, to believe that we are **chosen**. God really wants to use all of us in the ministry of building His kingdom. Totally amazing!

In fact, more like **Amazing Grace.**

> **I Corinthians. 1:26-31**
> "Remember, dear brothers and sisters, that few of you were wise in the world's eyes, or powerful, or wealthy when God called you. Instead, God deliberately chose things the world considers foolish in order to shame those who think they are wise. And he chose those who are powerless to shame those who are powerful. God chose things despised by the world, things counted as nothing at all, and used them to bring to nothing what the world considers important, so that no one can ever boast in the presence of God. God alone made it possible for you to be in Christ Jesus. For our benefit God made Christ to be wisdom itself. He is the one who made us acceptable to God. He made us pure and holy, and he gave himself to purchase our freedom. As the Scriptures say, 'The person who wishes to boast should boast only of what the Lord has done.'" *NLT*

What Happens When We Explore Amazing Grace?

When I first started my journey with the Lord I felt like it was the beginning of understanding God's call in my life. I call them my "formative years." I realized that I didn't have very much to offer God. This is not a bad place to start, because the concept never changes. We never have anything to offer Him, but He gives us everything we need to follow Him.

We often think we are supposed to meet up to some standard, or that we must be perfect if we are going to be used by God. This kind of thinking produces in us the attitude that we have to be or do something to experience the favor of God. We are sure we could never be really spiritual until we have achieved perfection. Another term for this kind of thinking could be called LEGALISM.

We will never figure out why the Lord calls simple people like us and uses them to do his ministry, but He does. I remember a time when I was going to speak to a group of women. I was sick for several days with diarrhea. This was two days before I would be speaking at this particular retreat. I had convinced myself that I didn't know much; I wasn't a trained speaker, I didn't look like a speaker. It was ridiculous! I wanted to just forget it. I wondered, 'Why in the world did I say I would do this?' I kept thinking that I had to meet up to some special kind of standard in order to be approved by God.

II Timothy 2:15
"Work hard so God can approve you. Be a good worker, one who does not need to be ashamed and who correctly explains the word of truth." *NLT*

I finally came to the conclusion that I was already approved by God. I had done my homework. I knew the Scriptures. But I was still worried about the approval of man. I was confused in my thinking. I was not living like a person with **grace** in my life. I had forgotten that the person I needed to please was the Lord and He would be offering me grace when I felt inadequate. This was phase one of *understanding His grace being active in my life.*

Intellectually I understood all the Christian jargon, "He will equip us for the work that He calls us to do," but I now had to test the validity of this statement.

I was getting ready to do a retreat. His work! He had gifted me to do His ministry to the body of Christ. I would be teaching and using my gift to build up the body of Christ. God's grace would be present in my life, but I had the pre-conference jitters. I was being attacked by fear. I had to get beyond my junk so I could do the thing God had called me to do.

The evening of the retreat, I put on and wore a pair of the wildest, craziest socks you could have ever imagined. They did not match one thing I had on in color or pattern. I honestly thought, "If I can wear these **outlandish socks then I can do anything**"...so I named my socks "**Jesus I Can Do Anything**" socks.

When something difficult or scary comes up, or I have to do something hard, I put on a pair of my socks. I have purchased socks that actually hurt your eyes to look at them. The pattern is crazy and wild, and never mind the color!

The socks became a visual aid to me. They reminded me that the Lord would be with me, He loved me, He had called me. His **Grace would be sufficient for me**. Where this idea came from, I can't say for sure. I only know that it helps me to focus on God and not my fears. This little visual aid became what I used to remind me that God would be there for whatever difficulty I was experiencing.

I now run around doing all kinds of things but I am wearing my "**Jesus I can do anything socks.**" I have bought them for my granddaughters for days when they are taking tests...I have gotten them for my sons...Dan wore a pair the day he had to appear in court. A person had run into his car and he had to go to court...He wore them to remind him that Jesus would be with him that day. I am now wearing, "**Jesus I Can Do Anything Underwear**" for days when you just can't wear the socks. I am reminded that it doesn't matter what I am doing or where I am going...Jesus and his GRACE will be with me.

I know it sounds like this is using a mental crutch, and we should just trust in God's word and that should be all we need. But sometimes we're not trusting. I am weak, I admit it. So you can wear your socks and know you are either crazy or your faith goes beyond natural thinking. Whatever! But I see this as the amazing grace of God in my life because God uses the weak and the feeble and fearful. And God uses this to bless me!

Now when I go to women's retreats I show up wearing my wild socks on Friday evening. I wish you could see the looks I get as I go to my retreats. I am sure they think to themselves, "What kind of speaker is she going to be?" Now I just have fun with it and I actually enjoy watching the eyes roll and the looks of total amazement.

I don't look like the polished retreat speaker that most of them expect. I am an ordinary person, very ordinary...like them, serving the Lord, not in my own strength but in the strength He provides, and wearing my socks while I am at it. I am living out my life as a person who has experienced the **grace of God**. Not very profound but real. When we understand **grace** our lives take on new meaning.

Living Life with Grace in Place

The definition of grace...grace is undeserved favor. It is mercy that we don't deserve or expect. He supplies us with an extra portion of understanding and compassion, and when this act of grace is in place we can do amazing things.

As we start to understand God's grace in our lives we cango beyond our puny self-centered thinking. We move into the area of walking in step with the Spirit. We begin to express compassion instead of disgust, hope instead of despair, freedom like nothing we ever thought or imagined. I am talking about "keeping in step with the Spirit", with our **Jesus I Can Do Anything Socks** on our feet. This is really **walking in the Spirit**.

> **Psalms 84:11**
> "He gives us grace and glory. No good thing will the Lord withhold from those who do what is right." *NLT*

This is the kind of grace God gives even when we haven't always been right or faithful. He gives grace when we have fallen into sin and he rescues us because He wants to demonstrate to us the truth about His character. He just wants to show us how much He loves us. This does not mean that God approves of sin, but we can sin and still be used by God again. Peter is a prime example of God's grace in his life; and Jonah is as well.

Ephesians 2:8-9

"God saved us when we believed. For by grace we have been saved, it is a gift, through faith, not of ourselves...because we might boast...We simply thank him and move on." *NLT*

The law was given to remind us that we cannot please God by anything that we do on our own. The law in fact showed us our sinfulness. He is pleased when we accept His grace and live out our lives **with grace in place**. We serve Him, not because we must but because we want to. Our hearts are drawn to Him and we love Him.

When **grace is in place**, it will
TRANSFORM OUR THINKING.

When we start to grasp His unconditional love, the Spirit of God surrounds us with security and peace. When the fruit of the Holy Spirit starts being freed up in our lives He is unleashed to do His work in our lives first and then we are released to share this truth with others. When we sin we pour water on the Holy Spirit; then His Spirit is quenched. We need to confess our sin and move on to the next stage. When God's grace is active in our lives we will be living in freedom. Freedom is expressed by the fruits of the Spirit: love, joy, peace, gentleness and kindness. We begin to move from our insecure selfish thinking into an openness to his thinking. What do you want me to do, where do you want me to go? How do I get there from here, God? **Where are those socks? I need them today!** I am ready to walk in freedom with the Holy Spirit released in my life.

Grace in Place produces ACTION! We begin moving and doing the things that God has equipped us to do. We start growing into the person that Christ has called and empowered us to be.

Galatians 6:1-5

"Brothers, (and Sisters) if someone is caught in a sin, you who are spiritual should restore him gently. But watch yourself, or you also may be tempted. Carry each other's burdens, and in this way you will fulfill the law of Christ. If anyone thinks he is something when he is nothing, he deceives himself. Each one should test his own actions. Then he can take pride in himself, without comparing himself to somebody else, for each one should carry his own load." *NLT*

I often ask people what they think it means to be spiritual. I have received many different answers. It usually has to do with what they will be doing for Christ, what they have done, or what they are doing right now. I suggest that being spiritual means remembering your roots, remembering that you are a sinner saved by **grace**, remembering that Christ forgave all the sins you committed before you became a Christian, all the sins you have committed as a Christian and all the sins you will commit ten years from now. We are now ready for the next step of action **bathed in Grace**.

- *Carry each other's burdens*. That is what we do as spiritual people. We are about the ministry of reconciliation. We are about helping restore others when they have been deceived and need help getting back on the path. Putting on our **socks and helping others put on their socks**. It's spiritual!

- *Carry our own loads*. We know where we have been and what we are about. But have we started the process of allowing God to recycle our junk? When we understand what it means to live as a forgiven person then we carry our stuff directly to the only One who can restore and heal us.

When we understand that truth for ourselves, then we can help someone else carry their hurt and pain to the Lord. We can expect His grace to be available for us. We have looked at our needs and we have experienced grace, and now we can come along side in the lives of our friends. This life in Christ is about experiencing Him for ourselves and then sharing it with others. The fellowship with others is so sweet.

HEALING GRACE now comes into focus when **grace is in place**.

The past, the pain of where we have been often tries to dominate our lives. We all have pain because we live in a fallen world. Sin would like to dominate our thinking but we will not be controlled by it. "Greater is He that is in us than the prince of this world." God begins replacing the shame and the blame with hope. The ministry of reconciliation becomes active.

We experience His grace and we then are able to extend grace to others. Guilt and discouragement have controlled our lives to a point that we believe this is normal. It is not! This new-found freedom starts to help us move forward, walking in the Spirit, free to be who we are **in Christ**. Remember that phrase from Chapter One. We have been immobilized, tranquilized and on a shelf until we begin to understand that God wants to heal our broken hearts. He wants to restore us and give us the ministry of restoring others.

2 Corinthians 5:18-21
"For God was in Christ, reconciling the world to himself, no longer counting people's sins against them." *NLT*

This is the message that gives hope for our own sin. We then can take this message of hope to others.

Romans. 5:1-2
"Therefore, since we have been made right in God's sight by faith, we have peace with God." NLT

Reconciliation with God comes through the faith process and brings about peace in our hearts. We are healed by His grace. Applying this healthy pattern is a powerful tool that can be ours, all who are in Christ. We then can start to appropriate His **healing grace** for our lives.

When **grace is in place**...
MARRIAGES ARE RESTORED.

I remember a time shortly after my husband passed away. I was given the name of a young man who would be my accountant and help me through the mess of sorting out the papers, the income tax information, all the financial aspects involved in losing a mate. The things you do not know can cause you pain. Dealing with all the legal details and records can add to your grief. It is a very difficult time.

I was in better shape than many widows, but there was so much I didn't know. And frankly, I needed a person to help me. This young man went through my checks, my shoe box full of papers. I simply kept some of my stuff in a paper bag. I gave it all to him to go over first. And then he came to my house to discuss these legal details and records. After some time I was ready to sign the final papers for the IRS for that year. He was able to comment that he knew I was really a Christian because of my check book. I thought that was interesting. But he was insightful and aware of Christian principles.

He and his wife had been divorced for six and one half years.

He had never remarried and neither had his former wife. He had been involved with other women but just never married. I could see he loved his children dearly. I asked him one day if he still loved his wife. He paused, looked me in the eye and told me he still loved her but they just couldn't seem to get along. I visited with the children from time to time and learned that they prayed all the time for their mom and dad to get back together again. I began to pray too. I began to think about the barriers there might be in this situation. What was keeping them from getting back together? I wanted so much for this marriage to be healed. It became apparent to me that they needed to learn how to forgive one another and to extend grace to each other.

Eventually I began meeting with his former wife. She had become curious about me because during that time the children enjoyed coming with their dad to my house and to my workplace at the radio station. They had even visited my church. I was able to spend some time with Clare just talking and sharing. I listened and I prayed. As our relationship developed we had many conversations in person and on the telephone. After some time I was able to meet with Tom and Clare together. Later the children joined us. I began to see healing between them as a result of these hours spent together and sharing the Word with them. The Holy Spirit was at work. We talked about a lot of things, and then I asked Clare one day if she still loved Tom. She was able to say "yes."

Investing our time in others for their healing is a ministry of God that we can be involved in. I will never forget the day they were remarried at the radio station where I worked. My pastor married them. They now have a new child in their family and they are still forgiving and still giving grace to one another. God can do anything when grace is in place. When healing grace is allowed to pour over us, and the freedom to forgive has its full reign in our lives, we can receive healing. It replaces the brokenness.

Whatever it takes to remind you that God is on the throne... and that He is still in control...do it. I wear loud **socks**...I know other people who wear them too. It is acceptable if we need a visual aid to remind us of **God's grace** in our lives. He wants to extend grace to us on a daily and hourly basis.

Consider This:

1. Can we still sin in spite of the grace of God?
2. How do you know God has extended grace to you?
3. What is it that you are not able to release to God so you can experience His forgiveness?
4. How long will you withhold your love from another person because you have been hurt and mistreated by them?
5. Do you think one of the reasons we have such a hard time forgiving one another is because we don't see it modeled very often? Who models forgiveness for you?
6. When are you going to get those loud socks?

_____

_____

_____

_____

_____

Chapter Four

CARING COMMUNICATION

Sticks and stones may hurt my bones, but words can never hurt me...

How many times have you and I been wounded by words? Wounded by words deliberately lashed out at us. Words simply dropped into the air but delivering a piercing blow to our hearts. How many times have we been disappointed by words not spoken? Marriages and relationships are fragile. Words spoken, or the lack of words when needed, can either hold us together or destroy us. We are confirmed or denied by words!

Caustic Words

Sometimes words spoken can eat at our emotions like an acid. I think one of my survival tactics in the past was my ability to produce those caustic words. Hurtful caustic words. If my words could throw someone off guard then I would still be safe. Little one liners. Phrases that I knew were clever, and partially true. Words that would eventually damage and destroy. Just enough of the truth to be dangerous.

I came from a neighborhood where, if you were small, you had better be either clever or a fast runner. You could often survive if you had a sharp tongue and were a cut-throat with words. Those sharp cutting returns could be a real asset in holding your own. My neighborhood was at times a verbal battle field. God is aware of this human trait. His Word tells us so.

> **Proverbs 11:17**
> "Your own soul is nourished when you are kind. but you destroy yourself when you are cruel." *NLT*

> **Proverbs 12:6**
> "The words of the wicked are like a murderous ambush, but the words of the godly save lives." *NLT*

We can actually bring healing to people with our words.

> **Proverbs 11:9**
> "Evil words destroy one's friends; wise discernment rescues the godly."

Many times I have sat with couples around a table over coffee... hearing over and over again..."She doesn't listen to me." "He doesn't say nice things to me anymore." "We seldom talk about anything but the bills." "She talks more to her friends than she does with me." "He yells at the kids and at me." "I don't know him anymore....we never talk." We know that communication, or lack of it, is a serious force in the break-up of marriages.

Proverbs 10:10-31,32

"People who wink at wrong cause trouble, but a bold reproof promotes peace. The words of the godly lead to life; evil people cover up their harmful intentions. Hatred stirs up quarrels, but love covers all offenses. Wise words come from the lips of people with understanding, but fools will be punished with a rod. Wise people treasure knowledge, but the babbling of a fool invites trouble. The wealth of the rich is their fortress; the proverb of the poor is their calamity. The earnings of the godly enhance their lives, but evil people squander their money on sin. People who accept correction are on the pathway to life, but those who ignore it will lead others astray. To hide hatred is to be a liar; to slander is to be a fool. Don't talk too much, for it fosters sin. Be sensible and turn off the flow! The words of the godly are like sterling silver; the heart of a fool is worthless. The godly give good advice, but fools are destroyed by their lack of common sense...

vs. 32 The godly speak words that are helpful, but the wicked speak only what is correct." *NLT*

Calming Words

Have you ever found yourself in a crisis? Of course you have! My definition of a crisis is anything that happens in my life that upsets my normal routine. It can be major or minor, but in my life some of the **circles of change** that keep coming around place me in the midst of some sort of crisis. And at times like these, calming words delivered in love can give us hope if we are able to receive them.

When my husband and I were told that unless something happened in the form of a small miracle he had only six months to live, I was numb.

I remember the doctor saying to us, "There isn't anything more I can do for you. Get your life in order, do and **say the things you need to say** so as to enjoy your days together." We were stunned. In fact, it took us a few days to grasp what the doctor had really said to us. It was right before Christmas and I wanted to call all of our children and demand that they spend the holidays with us. But Bill said, "Mom we need to spend this time together. There will be Christmas's that will be sad and lonely. We need to talk this out." And that is exactly what we did. I had no idea what was ahead for our family.

We sat at home in our snug little English Tudor home by our fireplace and just talked about our lives. All that week we talked and cried and just sat and held hands. We called our children on Christmas day. We visited with all of them on the phone. We chatted with our grandchildren and tried so very hard to be normal. I wanted to scream at them and scream at God. But nothing was going to change. Somehow, I knew this was it. The lot had been cast. I had not been asked for a vote, and God was going to take my Billy home... and very soon.

Even today, as I am typing these words and thinking about **calming words**...I am crying. I am sad. There is a peace that comes into our lives in spite of our circumstances. It doesn't mean that we are not sad, it just means that in the midst of it, we have His peace. I can tell you, I wore my **socks** nearly every day. I kept working and trying to deal at the same time with what I knew was inevitable. It was a terrible, stressful time. I do not know how I kept working and functioning as I did. My friend, Shannah Evans was a great help to me during this time. **She listened**. She has since gone home to be with the Lord in the circle of changes that was her life, but in our times together she allowed me to cry. To have someone listen as you share your heartache can be very calming. I have to admit, she allowed me to be cranky, too.

In February our doctor in Minneapolis called and told us about a laser procedure he could perform that might help Bill and give him a little more time. The blockage in his heart was serious. Each day it was closing down the possibility of the heart being able to function in a normal way. The time was passing so quickly.

Our doctor simply would not give up on Bill. But he knew the laser surgery would only buy time. He was concerned that Bill would need bypass surgery again. He had also contacted another doctor in Milwaukee, Dr. Dudley Johnson, who performed an unusual surgical procedure that went beyond the regular bypass surgery for heart patients. Bill's doctor was hopeful that he would be willing to take Bill as a patient. Dr. Johnson only took patients that were considered hopeless. People like Bill were waiting in the wings from all over the United States and other countries as well. Dr. Johnson would only consider you as a patient if you did not drink and you did not smoke; otherwise, what good would his surgery be if you would not try to live in a healthy way? Bill was also asthmatic and a diabetic, so lots of health issues were involved.

It was a brief moment of hope that sounded good. But it also was very plain to me that unless God came to the rescue...Bill was going home.

This is from a letter dated March 1, 1993. This letter was our prayer letter that we sent to our prayer partners.

"The card on the potted azaleas read, "From your

friends at Fond du Lac" We were both especially happy to learn, in this way, of the caring thoughts of my fellow workers at the school. Our trip to the St. Paul-Ramsey Medical Center had been brief and comfortable.

To be with us the three days in St. Paul, our son Michael had completed a long and hazardous journey from St. Louis to Cloquet through a fierce winter storm. We were grateful for his jolly presence with us—especially with Edna, while my cardiologist completed the cardiac cauterization procedures. An aortic balloon was inserted through the left femoral artery to the aorta, where it was inflated and used as a pump to safeguard the heart operation during the rest of the work. A laser and micro balloon were inserted through the right femoral artery to open and clear channels in blockages in the left anterior descending artery and elsewhere as possible. After two blockages were successfully cleared in about two and half hours, Dr. Topaz could proceed no further. The other blockages were calcified and could not be safely or successfully addressed. Both Dr. Topaz and my Duluth cardiologist Dr. Tekler, are making arrangements for me to be treated in Milwaukee, Wisconsin's St. Mary's Hospital, by a specialist named Dr. Dudley Johnson. He will be asked to do a triple coronary bypass within the next four to six weeks maximum. Doctors Topaz and Tekler will also be seeking MEDICA, Edna's insurance provider, to cover the associated costs. We do not know what their determination will be.

These doctors have told Edna that 'He is a heart attack waiting to happen. Because of the nature of the problem, if it happens up here there will be no one able to help him.' These are caring and respected physicians. I value their wisdom, skill and counsel. I also know who the Enemy is and what he wants to do. He wants us to fear. He does not want us to complete the assignment our Lord has commissioned us to do among our friends and fellow workers at Fond du Lac.

Pray for us as we continue our daily responsibilities in the strength God provides. Pray that whatever dollars are needed to restore me to stable health will be provided—through insurance or some other of God's purses. Pray that HIS NAME will be exalted."

We were very thankful that our son, Michael came up to go with Bill and I to Minneapolis where the laser surgery was going to be performed. By this time, I believe each of our sons had begun to grasp the seriousness of their father's health problems. Bill had always been positive because we had experienced many of God's miracles in our lives. We expected God's grace to give him some "slack" as Michael referred to it in his father's memorial service.

We went back to Cloquet where we waited. Michael went back home to his own set of problems and we all just tried to wait and see. Bill and I had many, many hours of conversation. I have never cried so much for so long in my whole life. I can remember Bill's words over and over again. "All of our days have been ordained by God"...each day is a gift and He alone knows the number of our days. These words had some comfort for me, but in my heart of hearts I knew this was not good. Bill would say, "You can't go before your time."

Finally, we were scheduled to fly to Milwaukee. Our middle son Tim was driving up to meet us there. Tim looks more like his father than Mike and Dan. Tim, is a very calming person. He was coming to help me with his dad. He had not seen his father for a time and I am sure it was a shock to see his father so pale and frail.

Naturally, Bill's health conditions had been very complicated. It was difficult to watch. For some time he had been popping nitroglycerin pills just to walk from one place to another. How he had managed to work up until the Friday before we flew to Milwaukee I do not know. But he had commented on the plane as we flew from Cloquet to Milwaukee, "Either way I win." "You're right, Turkey Butt," I said to him. In my heart I knew I would also win, but what a price! There was more to this life than our experience here on this earth. But life just went by too quickly. I knew we would always be together because of a previous commitment we had made in our hearts. We had both asked Christ to be our Savior and we would never be separated in eternity. We had the comfort of our faith and God's faithfulness to His word.

We moved on from the airport and to the hotel where we would spend the evening before Bill would be admitted. Bill's pain and discomfort was so evident. He was a very sick man. That evening before Bill was admitted to the hospital we celebrated life. Tim and Bill had their favorite, Chinese food...and a hot fudge sundae. No, it was not Bill's normal diet, but we choose to celebrate this precious time together.

The next day was Easter Sunday and we were reminded of the hope we have as believers. Resurrection Sunday! We believed that indeed God was in control and that nothing could happen to us outside of his will for our lives. I still believe that today. I count on it.

The surgery started early in the morning. They came out about three hours later and told us they had found a serious infection and that they had to partially close Bill up without doing anything because if they continued, the infection would spread through the chest cavity to his heart. He was returned to the ICU. When he came to, obviously he thought it was over and that the surgery had been a success. I had to tell him the truth.

He was placed on a high dosage of antibiotics, along with the steroids he was dependent on. They were postponing the surgery until the infection got under control. They believed he had been living with this infection since his by-pass surgery three years prior to this time. Bill had been in the hospital 17 times during the past three and one half years. It was frustrating to learn that the infection had never been identified during all of that time.

So Bill and I waited in the hospital. We talked a lot. I talked and he smiled and listened. Our kids came to see us on weekends and they called and told us how much they loved us, and they prayed. Bill's brothers came and spent time with me, as well as Bill's mom. She sat and held his hand when he was later in Intensive Care.

Tim's wife, Lois, our daughter in-love, is a nurse. Even though she is not a surgical nurse she knew the seriousness of the situation and constantly encouraged and prayed for Dad. He talked with her on the phone from the hospital. He would tell her what he thought was going on concerning his care. Bill liked to keep up with whatever medically was happening to him. Bill was very alert and was conscious of God's care in his life. I believe he was aware of God's presence in his life when he was in the coma for two weeks as well.

Michael would come up on the weekends with Tim and Lois, and then finally Dan and his wife, Dede flew in from Phoenix, so we were all together. It was a blessing to have our family with us. I needed them so much. We had a dear sweet couple from our home church in St. Louis that had moved to Milwaukee, Jim and Judy Wood. As a physician, Jim was helpful in interpreting what the staff told us. They looked in on me and cared for us every day. They also provided housing for family as needed.

Things were going well...then Bill started having an actual heart attack. The doctors agreed the surgery could no longer be delayed. **We prayed. It was in the Lord's hands.** Bill and I knew this was Show-Time. We could only hope that the medicine had cleared up the infection.

Our children came from St. Louis again. We waited the whole day. The surgery was a success, a seven by-pass procedure with two endarterectomies. Everything seemed as though he had made it, we had made it. Bill came out of the surgery and was only on the respirator for twenty-four hours. This was what I had expected of God, what we had prayed for.

We were so excited when Bill moved up to the 5th floor. It was a wonderful day. There were 12 families of patients with whom I became friends during the one month stay in Milwaukee. **Moving up to five** for us had become a statement of health, survival, promotion. At that time there would be a celebration in the cafeteria and all visitors rejoiced and thanked God for that family's good fortune. It meant that you could soon be going home. A close community developed and we all needed each other. Horrible events in our lives can bring total strangers together in an unusual way.

So we were ready. I remember thinking, we had survived the

worst time of our lives. We are going to be OK. We can start over again. Bill has this great new heart and our lives will be normal. Living with a diseased heart for so long had taken its toll on Bill, but it had also affected me as well. I had lived every day for so long, wondering when I got home from work if he would be alive. The times I had said good-bye to Bill were traumatic.

We were to fly home on Sunday, and this was Friday. It happened so quickly. Bill had required steroids to compensate for asthma for years. His adrenal system had been altered and high dosages were required to get him through surgery. This infection had been masked by the steroids and was not seen in his blood analysis. As the steroid levels were lowered for recovery, the killing infection had done its deed. His death certificate stated Toxic Shock Syndrome as the cause of death. I still cannot believe it.

I asked the questions, Why? Why? Why? God could have cleared up the infection. It was the means that God used to take Billy home to be with himself.

> *The calming words came to me over and over again...that nothing happens to us that our God doesn't know about....and the last words Bill spoke to me were, "I love you....will you be OK?" I said to him, "I'll be OK."...embrace whatever is happening to you .*

We had talked about this place in time, this moment that might come into our lives and now I was living it. We had discussed it clearly and normally, like you might be talking about a grocery list, but now, it was here. We were facing the final day! The Big Time Test of our true faith. This was it! We had both declared that no matter what seemed to be going on, we would trust God and His character. We would know that we were in His safe keeping.

We had calmly discussed what it would be like if God chose to take one of us home. *Till death do us part* had a significant meaning to us both. We were in this for the long haul. You cannot imagine this time in your life until you actually are forced to live through it. It is never gentle or kind. It is abrasive to your soul and you cry and yell and pray.

We will trust in the Character of God. I can tell you, those words have come to me in the middle of the night in the months and years that have followed my husband's homegoing. I have felt so alone and fearful at times, but in spite of it all...I know that He cares. God has been so merciful to me. Sometimes it will be a verse of Scripture that comes to my heart that causes me to be comforted. Sometimes it is a person that God sends my way to minister to me. Sometimes it is the peace of God that comes by way of the Holy Spirit. He lifts my spirit when I am low and I know it comes from Him.

Laugher has been part of my healing process. He has brought people into my life that have brought me laughter. People that you would never think could give you that gift, but there they were, sent by God. My emotions seemed to have died for a while. It was like something of myself died when I lost my husband. I didn't die and I was very much alive and I had to keep on working, eating, sleeping and being normal. I didn't do very well with this, as I reflect upon it, but I don't think anyone knows exactly how grieving should be done. Grieving is a different process, and we each experience it in a different way. And then, the Holy Spirit came along side of me in such a sweet way. He took me through the **circles of change, and he has brought peace to my hear**t.

The calming words come to me from time to time. I still need to hear them and I need to be reminded occasionally that yes indeed I will be okay. I am okay for now.

Communication and Listening

I think at times that we have forgotten how to converse with one another. I believe it is easier to think our thoughts and to be quiet than to honestly talk things through. We believe that children should be seen and not heard. We believe that if there is a problem, we shouldn't talk about it. We just move on as though nothing has happened. I am a communicator. I want to hear what has happened to you and I want to tell you what has happened to me. I want to share with you my resource. I want to tell you how God has taken me through the difficult times. I want you to know what has helped me. It is hard to talk about some things but it is the **caring communication we need to hear.**

I have heard many things over the years in counseling and caring for people. I don't think there's anything more I could hear that would shock me. I have listened to people as they have shared with me about their lives and seem to be stuck. No progress for years, then finally something gets through to them and they start to feel hope. God gives them hope. I have not liked what I have heard sometimes and it takes discipline to listen to people. We cannot fix them. Only God can bring healing into their lives. We need to communicate with others of God's faithfulness to us and encourage them to believe that God will also be faithful to them. We need each other in this way.

I think of how God created us for the purpose of having fellowship with us. He waits for us to come to Him on a daily basis. A daily quiet time is so important in our relationship with Him. It is reading His word, praying and then listening to Him speak to us while we are meditating on what we have been learning. The still small voice of the Holy Spirit speaks to us and helps us in the decisions we make. The Holy Spirit is our Counselor and our Guide. He wants to show us the way that we need to walk. Communication is not just our talking to God, it is also listening to what He says to us as well. I am always surprised that God wants to be with me. God actually wants to spend time with me!

I don't understand why people don't at least try and talk things out. If you can't do it alone, get a Godly counselor to help you through the stressful times. I realize when trust is broken it is hard to open up those lines of communication again. That is when we have to allow God to be our stabilizer. When our world feels like it is falling apart around us, we must abide in Him.

> **1 John 3:18**
> "Let us love not in word or in tongue, but in deed and in truth." *NLT*

Our words and our deeds go hand in hand. Words of anger feed the quarrel. Words of kindness can defuse the pain. Listening shows respect. If I have any regrets in my parenting skills, it would be that I did not listen enough to what my children were trying to tell me. **I didn't listen enough**. I was always giving orders and trying to keep everyone on my schedule. I didn't know any better. I listen now to my grandchildren and I can tell you I am hearing wonderful and different things. Listening without agenda is a great gift. I love it when Josh or Christopher talk with me. I seem to relate better to the boys. I am starting to get to know Jonathan a bit better and I hope he will come to know that I want to listen to whatever he has to tell me. The girls are a different thing.

They tell me lots of things but I am not sure I understand most of it. I am at least learning a few things in my old age. I am getting to know the grand daughters, Jackie, Megan, Julie, and Natalie. They are bright and interesting. I enjoy our times together.

Criticism and Critique

How do we build one another up in the Lord? Sometimes it is by our deeds, sometimes by our actions. But our **words** are powerful. My husband used to tell me over and over again how with the Lord's help I could do anything. I believed him. I valued his words to me. When we tell children they are bad, then they will be bad. When we tell children that they are special, they believe it and they are special. Our words can condemn or build up.

Generally, when we have allowed bitterness to control our thinking it is because we do not feel worthy. We deal with feelings of insecurity. We can help others by reinforcing the positive things we see in their lives. We need to tell them they are valuable. We need to give words of hope to one another.

God tells us over and over again how much He loves us. He wants to build us up. Sometimes God uses us to give those verbal gifts of encouragement to one another. It is in His plan and purpose for us to use our words to build up the body of Christ in positive ways. One of the reasons we feel so lonely and depressed is because the voices of comfort and hope are not being heard. There are some voices expressing their opinions on self worth that are not necessarily positive. Voices that are saying we should not think too highly of ourselves. But we are to be balanced in our thinking. We tend to think negatively of ourselves, rather than to believe in what God says about us. "We are precious to him." Real love expresses itself with action.

Philippians 1:3-11

"I thank my God every time I remember you. In all my prayers for all of you, I always pray with joy because of your partnership in the gospel from the first day until now, being confident of this, that He who began a good work in you will carry it on to completion until the day of Christ Jesus. It is right for me to feel this way about all of you, since I have you in my heart; for whether I am in chains or defending and confirming the gospel, all of you share in God's grace with me. God can testify how I long for all of you with the affection of Christ Jesus. And this is my prayer; that your love may abound more and more in knowledge and depth of insight, so that you may be able to discern what is best and may be pure and blameless until the day of Christ, filled with the fruit of righteousness that comes through Jesus Christ—to the glory and praise of God." *NLT*

What a difference it would make if our conversations concerning others had the sole purpose of building us up in the Lord? It causes me to consider the Scripture that says:

Isaiah. 8:16

"I will write down all these things as a testimony of what the Lord will do. I will entrust it to my disciples, who will pass it down to future generations." *NLT*

As the Word is life-changing to us, we must pass it on to others so that it will have the same effect in their lives.

Maybe we need to stuff those **socks** in our mouths from time to time. Knowing when to speak and when not to speak. It can be a real indication of spiritual maturity, or just plain discernment.

Proverbs 25:11-12

"A word aptly spoken is like apples of gold in settings of silver. Like an earring of gold or an ornament of fine gold is a wise man's rebuke to a listening ear." *NLT*

Consider This:

There's a lot to think about when we think of our words. Our words can confront, calm or condemn us. We have to choose to give out caring words. We are responsible for all of the words that come from our mouths. I for one wish I could recall some of my words...Perhaps, we could confess our loose tongues and ask God to help us weigh our words before we speak them. We have to remember also that little ears are listening and we are often condemned when we hear our children quoting us word for word.

1. We could maybe do a word study from the Scriptures on the use of the tongue. Proverbs is a very good place to start.

2. We might practice listening when it would be so easy to speak.

_____

_____

_____

_____

_____

_____

Notes

Chapter Five

CALM VERSES THE STORM

Over the years, I have come to see that comparing stressful living to the idea of storms has given me a another way of looking at stress. I lived in fear of life's storms for many years until I realized that I could not change all the factors that brought about those stressful times. Sometimes I just had to choose how I would ride out the storm until the calm came again.

I am also cautious when there is a calm....What is coming next? What is God's agenda? When our children became too quiet it was a sure sign that I needed to look in on them because I could be certain they were planning or plotting. It brought me great happiness when they were just playing and having a good time. Even the calm can cause concern, or the waiting period in between the storms.

Some of my personal storms have names, very much like the tropical storms that hit our coastal areas from time to time. Some are just tropical depressions, some are full blown hurricanes. Let's look into His plan for us to take shelter during the time the storm hits.

- *Identify* what the stress is in your life; get a handle on it, learn to recognize it when you see it again. *Name the stress!*

- Some storms, when identified are all too familiar. These are the storms we have to take responsibility for. Stress develops because we have said "yes" to too many things.

- Other storms are identified as little whirlpools but if allowed to continue become full blown storms. Stress can make minor issues into major issues. The "little foxes" in the chicken coop cause real stress.

- Get in touch with your own feelings about what is happening. Some storms may just be "tropical depressions."

- Guard your own coastline. We may tend to worry about the storms others are facing and neglect to deal with our own stress. This can be hidden behind a personality that helps others, but doesn't deal with their own issues.

Before any problem can be dealt with, we have to identify it. Then we are able to look into what God's word says specifically about an issue. With that information, God's view on the subject, we can see that what is happening is part of the **process**.

I also have to remember that God is taking me through this situation based on his time frame, not mine. Coming through the storm may mean riding it out. And riding the storm out may feel like the **process** is taking too much time. I tend to want to jump in and hurry up what God is trying to do. When I try to give God my opinion, the **process** tends to take more time. God doesn't need my assessment of the situation. When our decision making process includes patience, it is better than when we run ahead of God's plan. If we make hasty decisions just to make the stress to go away, the result can be even more stressful. Have you noticed what lengths we will go to in order to make it go away?

When stormy waves break over us we need to learn to body surf. Often our eagerness to have the stress be gone can take us on another journey. We get tumbled by the surf and washed into the rocks. We then get off into distorted thinking which says, "If God really cared about me, I would not be called upon to deal with this matter." It is never simple! We have to make a choice to commit ourselves to being **part of the process**, and allow God to work with us and our situations until the calm comes. We have no control over when or how that will happen. We are faced with trusting God to be faithful to His character, which we can rely upon during any stressful time.

Romans 5:3-5

"We can rejoice too, when we run into problems and trials, for we know that they are good for us—they help us to endure. And endurance develops strength of character in us, and character strengthens our confident expectation of salvation, and this expectation will not disappoint us. For we know how dearly God loves us, because he has given us the Holy Spirit to fill our hearts with his love." *NLT*

What causes Stress?

Often the stress we are experiencing is of our own doing. It is not like this is a new concept to us, it is simple truth. We bring stress into our lives when we sin. We bring it into our lives with the painful harvest of reaping what we sow. Also, failing to trust in God causes stress for us emotionally as we worry. Stress and storms are not always the result of sin, but we need to consider that as a strong possibility.

The world we live in is full of opportunities for stress. We would like to forget that living life as it is today certainly can be stressful. Our American dream encourages double incomes to enhance our style of living. It's nice, but the pursuit of happiness can also be stressful. And think of the work we go through for the holidays. Who should we invite this time? Will the time with our families be good this year? Graduations, promotions, new babies... all are good things, but also stressful.

Not long ago, in the normal events of living life, while taking out the trash, I was complaining to God that I missed Bill. I was struggling with how hard it was to figure out what I should be doing. Now trash is not on my list of the most inspiring subjects to talk about, but it reminded me of how poor health robs us of even life's simplest activities.

It was in the early evening and I was carrying my trash can out to the street thinking about how Bill and I used to do this chore together. It was something we did together, even though his angina would be bothering him and he would sometimes have to pop nitro tablets in his mouth before the trash finally reached the street. It was our thing to do together.

After we deposited the trash at the curb, we would go into the house and have a cup of tea together, talking and discussing the events of the day. It was a soothing time for me. I could sit and tell Bill some of my concerns. Just talking with him had a calming effect upon me as a person. He didn't necessarily have all the answers but he listened and I knew he cared. This is one of the by-products of our marriage that I liked best, because Bill and I enjoyed a special friendship. The trash was not even the issue; it just brought the sense of loss to the surface.

Bill and I were best friends. And marriages are happier and healthier if the husband and wife are best friends. We need outside friendships, this is true, but we also need that special friendship unique to marriage. We can lose children, parents and grandparents, but it is not like losing a spouse. Children lose a parent. I had lost a companion.

Since Bill's death, dealing with normal life had become so unreal. I had the feeling of being totally alone and responsible for everything. The stress was so different. I was dealing with living life without the help of my best friend and it didn't feel good and I didn't like it. I felt angry, and being alone didn't help. It took a lot of my energy just to exist. I had never had to deal with anything quite like it.

❖ ❖ ❖ ❖ ❖

It was in the early evening and I was carrying my trash can out to the street.

Borrowing from a familiar theme, do you think that this is the only stress that can come from remembering to take out the trash? No, from this necessary task of life comes yet another way of dealing with stress.

The trash situation in Minnesota is so difficult. If you do not have the trash sorted just so, you could receive notes from the trash people. I am not kidding! Who wants to have your trash rejected? You could receive notes from the company saying, "you had better comply to these specifications, or your trash will not be picked up in the future." When we have reached a high level of stress, things that are normal become overwhelming.

Do you know what it feels like to know that your trash has been rejected? It feels like you are personally being rejected. You are being rejected based upon how well you did with your trash this week. This didn't set too well with me. In fact, it made me angry. It was just another area of stress that I did not deal with very well...not at all in fact. I hate trash. I hate having to empty trash, wash bottles, tear off labels, wash cans, smash cans, separate plastic from bottles, remove caps and besides, **Bill did the trash**. He had the patience for it. He felt the call to do something for the environment; preserving the earth, reclaiming the earth and putting things back into perspective. It was his calling, not mine.

This particular evening I was carrying out the trash by myself, yelling at God as loudly as I could. One good thing about living in Minnesota is that in the dead of winter, who will hear you?! They have their windows and doors closed. I don't want anyone to get the idea that I don't think there are a lot of other good things about Minnesota, but being able to yell and scream and having no one to hear you is certainly a good one. You cannot yell and scream in Missouri. Your neighbors will hear you and think you are some kind of "nut case."

This evening, I was telling God how I didn't like being alone, no one was ever going to love me, and I didn't think that a loving, caring God would allow this to happen to me. Basically, I was complaining about taking out the trash again. But sometimes the normal events of life we struggle with are often not the real issue. Look with me again at the insight that can be gained when we allow God to help us identify the stress.

The next day I drove into the driveway and realized that not only did I have to take the trash out, I also had to drag the empty trash can back to its place in my yard. If we do not deal with the issues of the day, including our anger, we carry those things into the next day and add to that day's stress. I now had to carry the empty trash cans back to the place where I kept the can so I could start gathering the trash again. I never once thought to be thankful that someone was taking my trash off and out of my life. I could be grateful that they took my trash, or that my trash provided someone with a job, maybe even several people.

I noticed a paper bag hanging out of one of the cans. I thought to myself, "This had better not be another complaint." I looked at the bag, written in pencil across the side of the bag was a big heart, and inside the heart it said "**God loves you and so do I**."...**your Trash Man.**

Now, isn't that just like God! **Stress comes when we fail to trust God and ask for help. I hate it when that happens!**

Stress comes when we fail to identify the problems that cause our stress. It can be things from our past, or false beliefs about ourselves or others. Sometimes dealing with the stress of today means that we have to release our past and the people who may have caused us pain. I have found that a lot of my stress has been because I can't let it go. I keep digging up the past and adding it to what I am dealing with today. How foolish. Stress will cause us physical, emotional and spiritual pain if we do not look at it honestly.

How can I deal with stress and pressure?
(THE STORMS)

2 Samuel 22:7
"But in my distress I cried out to the Lord...He heard me from his sanctuary; my cry reached his ears." *NLT*

I like this verse because David yelled too.

Psalm s 55:22
"Give your burdens to the LORD, and he will take care of you. He will not permit the godly to slip and fail." *NLT*

God was probably helping me carry out the trash and I didn't even know it.

Psalm 86:7
"I will call to you whenever trouble strikes, and you will answer me." *NLT*

Isaiah 41:10
"Don't be afraid, for I am with you. Do not be dismayed, for I am your God. I will strengthen you. I will help you. I will uphold you with my victorious right hand." *NLT*

Modern Day Quote from Edna Blake:
God cares for me while I am carrying out my trash!

Something of great value is gained through stress. Our true character is being developed. When we are trusting in the character of God...nothing can harm us When we suffer pain, or we go through trials we have a resource that the world doesn't know about. We can even scream and yell!

God will not reject us. We don't have to understand what is happening, but we do need to trust and obey. We know that God is developing our character as well as teaching us to trust Him for all the circles of our lives. We can ask for mercy if we do not have the strength to believe or move. We can ask for Him to carry us.

God can redeem the brokenness. God can wipe away all our sins. God restores the broken and God heals us in the midst of our storms. I remember times when the only positive thing I could do was to list my sins and confess them before God and ask for His help. We have to focus on living as a forgiven people, remembering that He really does love us. He wants to restore us and heal us in the midst of the storms.

> **Galatians 6:9**
> "Don't get tired of doing what is good. Don't get discouraged and give up, for we will reap a harvest of blessing at the appropriate time." *NLT*

I used to think that only obsessive-compulsive people had trouble with stress. Then I started thinking, could this be me? Stress isn't happening in my life because I missed doing something right. It is part of life. We need to be balanced in what we do, also believing that we cannot control the storms. We cannot even prepare for them. I know that they tell people who live near the coastal areas when a storm is coming to prepare for that storm, but as you know, we can never be totally prepared. I knew that my husband didn't have long to live at one point, but I was not totally prepared for the months and years ahead. I had to grow in that knowledge on a daily basis.

We must allow God to help us apply forgiveness to our lives, along with His grace! When we get freed up in our lives, we can worship and praise Him through the storms. God takes us through these difficult times to demonstrate His love for us and to reveal to us His perspective.

I used to worry about how I would ever survive the storms and stresses in my life. I am learning that I must continue to process these truths in my life.

> *Trust*...**Philippians 4:19** "My God shall supply all your needs." *NLT*

> *Be Patient*... **Psalm 27:14** "Wait on the Lord; be strong and take heart and wait for the Lord." *NLT*

> *Pray*...**1 Thessalonians 5:17** "Pray Continually." *NLT*

Prayer is not a quick fix, but many things can be resolved through prayer. It can change our attitude right on the spot. When the Spirit of God moves in our hearts and we see peace in the midst of the turmoil, it will encourage us.

> *Seek Godly advice*...**Galatians 6:2** "Bear one another's burdens, and so fulfill the law of Christ." *NLT*

Stress Is Multiplied
When We Have Problems with Others.

Learning the skills to deal with other people in our lives can be very stressful. When we have conflict with co-workers, family members, the other people in our church, neighbors, we want resolution and it doesn't always happen. This is not a blaming and shaming statement, it is simply how it is.

We need to commit to one another for the long haul. We need to deal with the people in our lives that cause us to be stressed. We need to also consider that at some point, **we are the people that cause others' stress**. When we try to meet the expectations of others and can't, we may need to set the healthy boundary and walk away from it.

I am a mom, a daughter, a grandmother, a mother-in-law, and a member of a local church. I can only deal with one person and one situation at a time. I cannot please all of these people or meet all of their expectations. We can only be certain of one thing, we need to please God. We can ask Him to help us relate more Christ like in our relationships but we will never be able to be perfect. We should try as much as possible to be at peace with all people, and acknowledge that we will not be totally successful in our attempts.

Conflict can be good as it causes us to examine the situation and possibly give us a different perspective. As we review the situation we may learn some things about ourselves. God may give us insights about ourselves that we never had before. This process may be stressful, but it still produces growth. Avoiding the stress of growing and developing in our relationships will dwarf the growth. Allowing relationships to stagnate will do no good. And wanting to be in control of the relationship, having the upper hand all the time doesn't work. Relationships that are healthy take time and commitment and a positive compromise. Sometimes the process of conflict brings us to an undesirable conclusion which is the fact that not everyone will like us, but it won't be the end of the world. Many times missionaries are not stressed by their mission or what they are doing in a different culture; they are stressed with trying to deal with the other missionaries. Acceptance of others who are different from us, who may think differently from us is stretching and stressful, but the process will promote maturity in us by the grace of God.

God's Guidelines For Coping with Stress.

Ephesians 5:10 "Find out what pleases God." *NLT*

Bitterness and unforgiveness give us our greatest problems in dealing with stressful relationships. We are to love one another. It is the foundation we have been given by God as His plan in helping us to relate to one another in a healthy way. If we do not find a way to deal with these broken relationships we end up living out our lives alone and with bitterness that will rob us of our peace and joy. When we choose not to forgive we are sinning. We quench the Spirit and we are on a path of self destruction. When we choose to hold on to a grudge we are sinning. Forgiveness must be a choice. It is hard on our egos at times but it is the right thing to do.

We face an additional problem when dealing with forgiveness. It is to be a deliberate act of will resulting in observable change. If we forgive, we must deliberately choose to behave as we have declared we would do. We have to let the transgression go and allow people the freedom to start again with us in the relationship. We have to release the anger. "True love seeks the loved one's highest good." Obedience doesn't always feel good. I have heard it said that only God can completely forgive. This is true, but He commands us to forgive others in the way He has empowered us to.

Matthew 5:43-47
"You have heard that the law of Moses says 'Love your neighbor and hate your enemy.' But I say, love your enemies! If you are kind only to your friends, how are you different from anyone else?" *NLT*

We need healthy boundaries in our friendships, but kindness and forgiveness can go a long way in helping us reduce the stress as it relates to our friendships. When we persevere in our friendships, we will choose to try and understand where the other person may be coming from. We can respect them even if we do not agree with their perspective. We know that acceptance of others will bring us into seeing them through God's eyes. I want grace for my life and I want to also extend grace to others. Forgiveness and grace seem to go hand in hand.

Reducing Stress And Its Effects Will Bring About Peace

The world is the way it is. I may be able to influence some part of it for change but for the most part, I need to **accept that I can only change me**, with God's help.

What are our motives, expectations, and desires? If we separate our "needs" from our "wants" we start to get a better perspective of understanding our own personality and what our value system might be. **We need to be honest about our motives**.

Facing our own contempt or prejudice prior to investigating what is really happening is a must. Be willing to listen to others objectively. We may not always be ready to listen fairly to others. We may need to do a quick reality check on our responses and behavior based upon what God says is the standard as revealed to us through his Word. In dealing with a conflict, if we are critiquing another person's life, we need a willingness to be corrected in our own behavior We might have a problem we need to do something about. This is a big issue in handling stress in our relationships and in our personal lives. I have a very good relationship with a longtime friend now. But we struggled and worked hard to get where we are today. Conflict resolution caused us to learn why we behaved the way we did. We accepted our differences, we forgave and forgave again. We learned not to hold grudges. We moved on to the next stage and the next set of problems. Because we made positive compromises we were able to work it through.

Perseverance. Being willing to stick to the problem until the calm comes. In relationships, **caring enough to confront** is what it is actually called. If I don't care about you then I will dismiss you and move on to someone else. A relationship stagnates when I do not care about what God thinks. How we treat others and deal with others will eventually affect our relationship with God.

Consider This:

If we do not deal with stress and storms, the effects will eventually come to our front door. They will come in the form of health problems. A term that has been redefined to apply to stress in the 80's and the 90's is burnout. The storms and stress will eat away at you. Workaholic will be an adjective used to describe your personality.

1. What steps can you take to start dealing with your personal stress?
2. Who will you tell about your stress? Will you consider telling someone about your feelings of stress so you can have someone pray with you about this situation in your life?
3. Is your stress temporary, or has it become a way of life?
4. How long has it been since you have been calm and peaceful? Your sleep will be destroyed if you continue to live under the bondage of stress.

Confess your part in living the stress-filled life. Don't let it be "just the way it is." You can change, you can choose, you can risk, you can fail. You can have victory in the Lord.

And don't forget: Put on those socks, so you will remember to relax in the Lord. You need to trust Him to get you through the next steps.

_____

_____

_____

_____

_____

Chapter Six

COME ON DOWN!

We have all seen the TV program that calls for the people from the audience to "Come on Down" because *now they will be a contestant.* They will no longer be sitting in the audience observing. They are now **called** upon to actually participate. They will be the contestant!

When you are watching one of those programs that ask questions have you noticed how many answers you know? If you were to actually become a contestant would you even be able to speak? Have you also noticed how the audience calls out the answers to the people who are the contestants? Can you imagine what it must feel like to actually be the contestant and have others screaming out the answers to you while you are trying to focus on the question?

Who should we listen to in those kinds of situations? How do we know which person has the right answer? Most of us would freeze on the spot and not even be able to speak. We could possibly even know the answers and not be able to think that quickly on our feet and lose our turn. We are **called** by God as believers to "**come on down**"...and live it out! We have to learn how to act decisively upon what we know and what we believe. This is where the "rubber meets the road."

Cookie Cutter Salvation

We all must come to Christ by way of the cross. We readily agree to knowing that as truth, but each of us experiences living out our faith differently. We are at different levels in our walk with Christ. We can both be growing at the same time while learning different truths. My mission field will be different from yours. I am called to share my faith in one way, while you are called to God's task for you in your area and in your work place. We are called to be conformed to the image of God, not each other.

Romans 8:28-30
"And we know that God causes everything to work together for the good of those who love God and are **called** according to his purpose for them. For God knew his people in advance and he **chose** them to become like his Son, so that his Son would be the firstborn, with many brothers and sisters. And having **chosen** them, he **called** them to **come to him**. And he gave them right standing with himself, and he promised them his glory." *NLT*

We have been clearly **called by God to share with the world**. This is a true statement, but we are **called first to belong to Him**. We cannot share with the world His salvation until we understand it for ourselves. We must first accept the gift of salvation for ourselves. It is personal. It is individualized. We can all have a personal relationship with God through His Son, Jesus. Our sin problem cannot be eliminated by any other way than taking the responsibility to respond to God's call in our lives. He wants to set us free from our sin.

When we accept this provision of salvation. We start a whole new life in Christ. Christians relate to God differently. We have similar experiences with the Lord, but not the same. We are taken by the Holy Spirit into areas that He calls us to and equips us for serving. We may be asked by God to follow Him as individuals, and at times He calls us to do something corporately. We as contestants are sometimes on the team, and at other times on our own.

At church potluck dinners, each cook will bring the dish that is their specialty? It is a wonderful time. Many people will make similar casseroles or desserts. For some events everyone will be asked to make the same dessert on purpose. All have used the same ingredients with the same recipe. But the finished product will look and even taste different, based on each cook's interpretation of the recipe.

We cannot compare ourselves with one another. God made us individuals and we are all unique. We talked about this in Chapter One. We have to remember that our model and example is Christ, not each other. Apply God's standards to our own lives first. Model what Christ means to us as contestants. Don't be influenced by the yelling crowds as to how we should respond to God's calling in our lives. We should listen to our own hearts with the guidance of the Holy Spirit.

1 Thessalonians 4

"Finally, dear brothers and sisters, we urge you in the name of the Lord Jesus to <u>live in a way that pleases God</u>, as we have taught you. You are doing this already, and we encourage you to do so more and more. For you remember what we taught you in the name of the Lord Jesus. God wants you to be holy, so you should keep clear of all sexual sin. Then each of you will control your body and live in holiness and honor—not in lustful passion as the pagans do, in their ignorance of God and his ways.

Never cheat another Christian in this matter by taking his wife, for the Lord avenges all such sins, as we have solemnly warned you before. God has called us to be holy, not to live impure lives. Anyone who refuses to live by these rules is not disobeying human rules but is rejecting God, who gives his Holy Spirit to you.

But I don't need to write to you about the Christian love that should be shown among God's people. For God himself has taught you to love one another. Indeed, your love is already strong toward all the Christians, in all of Macedonia. Even so, dear friends, we beg you to love them more and more. This should be your ambition: to live a quiet life, minding your own business and working with your hands, just as we commanded you before. <u>As a result, people who are not Christians will respect the way you live</u>, and you do not need to depend on others to meet your financial needs." *NLT*

Your experiences with the Lord may be similar to mine but I guarantee you, those experiences will not be the same. We learn to obey and walk with the Lord based upon our own relationship with God. I marvel over the fact that someone in India may be learning the exact thing I am learning from the Lord. God is so amazing.

<u>Living out our individual lives will be based upon how we grow and develop as a individual believers</u>. This life in Christ will be different and challenging for each of us. As team players or individuals we must play by the rules of the game.

Our Confidence must be in the Lord

When we shared about having **grace in place** in our lives we focused on the fact that God extends to each of us His favor and His grace. He also directs us and He deals with us according to His plan and purpose for our lives. We tend to want others to answer the hard questions for us. We don't want to do the homework. We want someone to tell us the easy way. What is the short cut for success? Forget it! We are now the **contestants** and we must answer the hard questions and we must be the responsible ones. **Come on down is about living out our faith**. It is about every day living and depending upon him.

How You Do That?

The international students asked that question of the American students many times. HOW YOU DO THAT? It became a joke on campus. Anytime a certain international student saw something he liked, **he wanted to know how he could learn to do that**. In other words, **teach me**.

2 Corinthians 1:8-11
"We do not want you to be uninformed, brothers, about the hardships we suffered in the province of

Asia. We were under great pressure, far beyond our ability to endure, so that we despaired even of life. Indeed, in our hearts we felt the sentence of death. But this happened that **we might not rely on ourselves but on God**, who raises the dead. He has **delivered us** from such a deadly peril, and **he will deliver us**. On him we have set our hope that **he will continue to deliver us** as you help us by **your prayers**. Then many will give thanks on our behalf for the gracious favor granted us in answer to the prayers of many." *NLT*

This passage of Scripture has some very basic teaching for us.

1. Do not rely upon yourself...but upon God.

2. Remember that He has delivered you....He will deliver you...and He will continue to deliver you.

3. Surround yourself with people who know how to pray for you. They will continue to uphold you in prayer even when you are out of sight.

We are all contestants....players for the Lord's team. Workers in the fields. Gatherers of the harvest. Disciple makers.

What is a Disciple Maker?

Making disciples is not an option. It is a Biblical mandate, Christ has called us to do this. It is the practical side of living out our Christian life. It is being a Christian, a contestant. It is a person who participates in the ministry of living the Christian life. It is about **coming on down**!

Matthew 28:18-20
"Then Jesus came to them and said, 'All authority in heaven and on earth has been given to me. Therefore go and make disciples of all nations, baptizing them in the name of the Father and of the Son and of the Holy Spirit, and teaching them to obey everything I have commanded you. And surely I am with you always, to the very end of the age.'" *NLT*

Jesus is commanding us as well. He is calling us "**to make and teach others, to train those He will send our way.**"

This very simple definition for understanding what is meant by making disciples. Paul discipled Timothy.

2 Timothy 2:2
"And the things you have heard me say in the presence of many witnesses entrust to reliable men who will also be qualified to teach others." *NLT*

- **Teaching others what we know of Christ and his teachings.**

- **Sharing our lives with others. We are to be examples and models of what Christ has done for us.**

Timothy experienced the pattern before Paul explained the process. More is caught rather than taught. Bill and I used to teach people about leading small groups, and the best way we found to teach this principle was to involve them in a small group experience. We must walk together through the process as growing disciples. We are in this together. It is important to rely upon the Holy Spirit as our teacher, but we need others to teach us and model these principles.

This is how the mandate works: I learn a principle from God's Word, I remember what I have learned, and then teach the concept to you. At some point the person who is being discipled will began sharing with you and they will teach you what they are learning. This is the stage that becomes very exciting. The light bulb goes on! Then both of you will join together and teach others.

Can you imagine the response Saul received from the Church when they first heard that he had become a follower of the way? He had persecuted the church. He had given the orders to kill many of the Christians. Some of their families were in the churches where Saul (now called Paul) was now preaching. He showed up telling them he was also a believer of the way. He began to teach them immediately what he understood about Christ and his experience with the Lord. They questioned among themselves, "Can this be true, or is this another one of his tricks to get us to betray the Lord and others of our way?" They must have listened very intently. They must have weighed his words and questioned everything he said. We would have questioned him too.

Barnabas came along side and brought Paul into the body of believers. Barnabas risked his reputation. He went out on a limb for Paul. He took Paul and brought him into the presence of the apostles, and told them about Paul's conversion and how he was preaching about Jesus. Barnabas in the beginning discipled Saul, and Paul discipled Barnabas back, then the two of them continued discipling and bringing others to Christ.

When we are only **observers** and not **contestants** we may have opinions, but it is only when we start participating in the game plan that God really uses us to proclaim His message. Serving Christ, of course, is not a game. It is fulfilling the call of

Christ upon our lives to **come on down and make disciples**.

Contestants are Tested

"Count it all joy when various testings and trials come into your life." Does that sound familiar? Well, maybe we don't feel like counting it all joy! Maybe we're just so overwhelmed we can only think in terms of making it through the trial. Perhaps that would be a more realistic approach as we ponder how to live out this "practical Christian life." Looking at our lives from a realistic point of view one day at a time, rather than trying to deal with a whole lifetime.

When we first became contestants, we believed in "Super Christians". They were the ones who could go through anything. We thought, They were the ones who were able to walk on water. They gave out this aura which allowed us to think they were beyond and above us. They seemed to have this positive testimony and a glib smile upon their faces. They not only see no evil, do no evil, they are so outstanding, we wonder, are they for real? There are no super Christians. We all have to be proven.

I remember when we lost our first baby. Thomas Andrew was not our first child but our fourth. We have lost two little boys. I had carried Thomas Andrew the whole nine months plus. Everything seemed to be normal. The whole pregnancy seemed normal, the delivery seemed to be very routine, but something was very wrong. Right up to the time he was to be born he was alive, but nothing could be determined or understood until after he was delivered. The baby's cord was around his neck and he never survived coming through the birth canal. I wondered and wondered, Why us? Why our baby?

I never considered myself as a person God would entrust with this kind of responsibility. I was just trying to survive being a pastor's wife serving in a small church, mother of three, and living in the parsonage - all normal things Christians experience.

I am not now or ever have been a "Super Christian". I was just trying to survive the best I could. It seemed like I just got to come up on stage and someone handed me the experience. It was a real experience in tasting grief and loss. I was taken by surprise by God's will for my life. I wasn't prepared but I soon discovered that God was with me. He sent others to come along side. It was a very difficult time in my life. It was difficult for our whole family.

Somehow, we survive. Make those peanut butter sandwiches, wash those clothes, carry in the fire wood, can those vegetables, read those stories to our children. We fill our time with busyness because it hurts too much if we take time to think about what we are actually experiencing because we can't stand to be quiet or alone. Our lives are thrown into turmoil and we have no idea what the next move might be for us. We are just trying to practice what survival skills we have learned.

Where do those questions come from? Why me, Why our baby, Why? I didn't know what I was going to do, or how I was going to survive. God's will often takes us to places we do not want to go. His plan and purpose doesn't seem to fit any of our plans. It was a crazy time! We all just stopped for a while trying to catch the next bus that would take us to the promised land, but we couldn't seem to find the schedule.

The loss of our fourth child came two weeks before Christmas. It is a busy time for the pastor and we were in the midst of "Joy to the World" and grief. This is the time of the year when you get to see all those people you hadn't seen since last Easter. It is a spiritual challenge and we were just trying to get through our grief.

A lot of things run through your mind when you are in the midst of grief. I remember praying the first time I felt the baby move inside of me. It is the time when you as a mother know this little person is a person. I prayed that if he would grow up and not know the Lord, God would take him home. I wanted all of my children to be saved. I never prayed that prayer for any of the others. I still do not know why I prayed that prayer in the first place, but I did.

In the hospital room after the delivery I remember how quiet it was. I never heard the baby cry and I knew he wasn't alive. The Sister who attended my birth was cleaning me up and fussing over me. I said to her, "The baby is dead, isn't he?" Behind her mask I could only see her eyes. She just shook her head yes. What could she say? Silence is a response.

Later, when I was in my private room, I remembered the prayer I had prayed months ago. I really don't think God was unkind or unjust at this point. I believe God was merciful. I do not believe I could live knowing that my sons rejected the provision of Christ for their sins. God was merciful when he took our baby home. It was a strange kind of comfort, but I knew that was the day I became **a real contestant, or it was the beginning of joining the ranks of those who have been disciplined by trials and testings**. Bill and I wanted our children to know Him. It is what all of us as parents desire for our children. When our sons grew up and made that decision for the Lord it was a great gift that God gave to us.

I came home from the hospital and it was a very different

kind of Christmas for all of us. Bill attended the memorial service along with some of the church members and it was just a hard time. Michael kept asking about when we would bring his baby home. I would tell him again how baby Thomas was in heaven with Jesus. Tim was confused by the fact that we kept talking about baby Jesus in the manger. Tim didn't know which baby we were talking about, our baby or baby Jesus. We told the children that Christmas was baby Jesus's birthday. Dan was smiling and happy. He had his Mom back from the hospital. He walked around the room and tried to be shy, then he ran and hugged me. It seemed like some sad tale you would read about in the life of a missionary, or in the life of some "Super Christian." Only it was us and it didn't seem anything super to me.

That Christmas taught me a great truth from the word of God. It was a time for me to finally understand and come to grips with the simple message of Christmas..."For God so loved the world that he gave His only begotten Son." He gave up His Son...for me, for my sin. God gave His only begotten Son. God gave His Son.. The concept of what that meant to God finally hit me. I had a small glimpse of what the real meaning of Christmas was about. I think of it every year and I believe it makes the season more special for me.

God's Contestants are Blessed

The Christmas of 1960 also had blessings. We had very little money after the funeral expenses and hospital expenses. Our church people had been very generous and helpful to us. But it was going to be a very slim Christmas as far as presents and gifts were concerned. We usually put up our tree on Christmas Eve, and we also opened our presents on Christmas

Eve. Bill usually got paid on Christmas and then we could purchase our tree. We had many wonderful "Charlie Brown Christmas Trees." I usually had most of our presents ready to be put under the tree, but this year nothing seemed to be in place.

Michael recited the Christmas story from Luke. We had been working on that for weeks. After the Christmas story, Bill would pray and thank God for Jesus, the best gift ever. We would then open our presents. Nothing too exciting or special, but this year, there was no tree. And the children would be getting only the presents from their grandparents. Tim kept interrupting as Michael was reciting the Christmas account of the birth of Jesus. "I hear some noise out on the porch. I know I hear something." Tim was not going to let it go. He heard noises and he wanted to know what he was hearing. After we prayed and thanked God for sending His son, Jesus, for helping us to get through this hard time, Bill finally went to the door and on the front porch was Christmas.

We still do not know to this day just who came to the rescue that evening. It was someone who knew our family, that was evident. A tree was there, fully decorated and ready to be plugged in, along with a box of food with the trimmings. There was a huge ham and everything to go with it. Boxes and boxes of presents. I looked at Bill and he looked at me. The boys were delighted. "Can we open them now?" God sent us a special gift that year. We learned about the reason for the season, and we learned that along with the testings and trials come the blessings.

The Contestant's Reward

1 Peter 1:3-9
"Praise be to the God and Father of our Lord Jesus Christ! In his great mercy he has given us new birth

into a living hope through the resurrection of Jesus Christ from the dead, and into an inheritance that can never perish, spoil or fade—kept in heaven for you, who through faith are shielded by God's power until the coming of the salvation that is ready to be revealed in the last time. In this you greatly rejoice, though now for a little while you may have had to suffer grief in all kinds of trials. These have come so that your faith—of greater worth than gold, which perishes even though refined by fire—may be proved genuine and may result in praise, glory and honor when Jesus Christ is revealed. Though you have not seen him, you love him; and even though you do not see him now, you believe in him and are filled with an inexpressible and glorious joy, for you are receiving the goal of your faith, the salvation of your souls." *NLT*

Blessings and rewards are different. Blessings can be for that one time. They will be remembered always, but rewards have to do with being honored, or given a special everlasting gift. It has to do with our inheritance.

- **Salvation, our new birth in Christ.**
- **Inheritance, that can never perish, spoil or fade.**
- **Sufferings for a little while.**

The trials and testings that come into our lives happen because God is in the midst of perfecting our faith. God is developing our faith through the various trials, the things that happen to us which cause us to give up our ideas and plans. Those things in our lives that force us to walk by faith and not by sight. We are required to trust and obey.

Grief plays a part in developing our faith. We are spiritually challenged in every area of our lives when we are forced to deal with grief. It is one of the ways we learn to truly love Christ. Even though we have never seen Him, we love Him and we believe in Him. Jesus is God's gift to us. Jesus in our lives gives us meaning and purpose. Knowing Christ is the first step in learning to **walk by faith**.

When we "**come on down,**" **we are ready to participate in God's plan for our lives**. "We are in the world but not of this world." The gift of faith is from the Holy Spirit. It is impossible to produce faith in and of ourselves. Faith is a gift to us. It is one of the fruits of the Spirit. When it takes hold of our lives we view ourselves and others differently. We need <u>faith working in our lives</u> as we make choices, which we have talked about in a previous chapter. We need <u>believing faith</u>.

> **Genesis 15:6**
> "And Abram believed the Lord, and the Lord declared him righteous because of his faith." *NLT*

We need <u>living faith</u>...the kind that is talked about in Hebrews II. What is faith? "It is the confident assurance that what we hope for is going to happen. It is the evidence of things we cannot yet see. God gave His approval to people in days of old because of their faith."

Consider This:

1. As a contestant, what hinders you from participating in the Christian life?

2. When you think about making disciples do you feel you are still a growing disciple and you need to be trained yourself?

3. What are some things you could do to be involved in discipleship training?

4. Do the testings you are experiencing cause you to persevere? We may never understand the test and we may never feel that we have learned anything from the experience, but the rewards have not yet been handed out.

Ask God to help you as you learn to walk by faith and not by sight, but be prepared to go through difficult times.

Notes

Chapter Seven

COURTING DECEPTION

None of us set out to be deceived. We don't wake up one morning and think to ourselves, "Today I want to be deceived." We somehow believe that we will escape falling into sin and being deceived. We believe we will somehow avoid the mistakes our parents made. We want to somehow escape the pitfall we have observed others making along the way. Somehow we believe we will do better. We will not make those mistakes and we will not be deceived. Those who remarry say to themselves, "This marriage will be different." Unless the patterns of behavior change, unless each person in the marriage determines with the help of God to be different, the same mistakes of poor judgment will again be repeated.

We must choose to make different choices. If we do not stop the deception we will again be deceived. The other side of the coin represents another part of the equation. If the deceived one does not stop the pattern they will also deceive others. It is a vicious circle. We can also fall into the trap of believing we have become so well informed that we will not get caught in sin. We certainly do not have as a goal for our lives to be deceived or to deliberately deceive others. We fail because of our natural inclination to sin.

When we allow deception into our lives we fall prey to the enemy's tactics. He wants to deceive us, and we are vulnerable. We must remember to put on the full armor of God daily. We have to start listening to the Holy Spirit when He confronts us with sin. We are the target for the enemy's devices. He knows all of our weak areas and he shoots the darts for the purpose of attack and disrupting our walk with the Lord. When we are not walking in the Spirit we will be walking in the flesh.

Highway trips are always interesting, but getting lost on the road isn't. Traveling somewhere new requires special attention to where we are going. But even a trip to a familiar but distant destination can find us lost. The roadways or landmarks may be unfamiliar or have changed since last we traveled that way. If we are not carefully paying attention to the signs, a tendency for losing our way can come into play. One good thing we ladies can do if this happens is to ask for directions. We can get out our map, or we can go back to the place where we started. We will eventually get back on track, headed for our destination.

Similarly, when we allow ourselves to be deceived it is often because we have not obeyed what we know to be the truth. Deception can be subtle. We can be deceived about things that have the appearance of good. We can look away for just a moment and miss the truth. We must be cautious and careful about how we deal with the enemy. Deception can be compared to missing the turn, allowing obstacles to block our view, not seeing the signs. In life, we can choose to take someone along with us, someone who knows the way and has traveled the route many times, a friend by the name of accountability.

How Can I Know When I Am Being Deceived?

I have spent some time thinking about the idea of being deceived and how that happens. We naturally think of Eve, but there are many examples in Scripture that give us examples of deception. One example in the Old Testament has a lot of intrigue and has always been one of my favorite stories. It is really challenging to read because of the validity of the story. It is the account of Samson and Delilah. The story is taken from the pages of Judges but the application for today's world is very real.

> ### Judges 13:1-6
> "Again the Israelites did what was evil in the Lord's sight, so the LORD handed them over to the Philistines, who kept them in subjection for forty years." *NLT*

In those days, a man named Manoah from the tribe of Dan lived in the town of Zorah. His wife was unable to become pregnant, and they had no children. The angel of the LORD appeared to Manoah's wife and said, "Even though you have been unable to have children, you will soon become pregnant and give birth to a son. You must not drink wine or any other alcoholic drink or eat any forbidden food. You will become pregnant and give birth to a son, and his hair must never be cut. For he will be dedicated to God as a Nazarite from birth. He will rescue Israel from the Philistines."

Samson had a good start. He had a wonderful family. His parents were devoted to him from day one. Perhaps this over-indulgence contributed to Samson's attitude. Parents often indulge their children to a point where the children assume that their parents are like God. The children start to believe that whatever they want the parents will get for them. Children left to their own thinking may believe they can have anything they want, and when they want it. HELLO!

Judges 14

"One day when Samson was in Timnah, he noticed a certain Philistine woman. When he returned home, <u>he told his father and mother, 'I want to marry a young Philistine woman I saw in Timnah.'</u> His father and mother objected strenuously. 'Isn't there one woman in our tribe or among all the Israelites you could marry? Why must you go to the pagan Philistines to find a wife?'

<u>But Samson told his father, 'Get her for me. She is the one I want.' His father and mother didn't realize the Lord was at work in this, creating an opportunity to disrupt the Philistines, who ruled over Israel at that time.</u>

As Samson and his parents were going down to Timnah, a young lion attacked Samson near the vineyards of Timnah. At that moment the Spirit of the LORD powerfully took control of him, and he ripped the lion's jaws apart with his bare hands. He did it as easily as if it were a young goat. But he didn't tell his father or mother about it! When Samson arrived in Timnah, he talked with the woman and was very pleased with her.

Later, when he returned to Timnah for the wedding,

he turned off the path to look at the carcass of the lion. And he found that a swarm of bees had made some honey in the carcass. He scooped some of the honey into his hands and ate it along the way. He also gave some to his father and mother, and they ate it. But he didn't tell them he had taken the honey from the carcass of the lion. As his father was making final arrangements for the marriage, Samson threw a party at Timnah, as was the custom of the day. Thirty young men from the town were invited to be his companions. Samson said to them, 'Let me tell you a riddle. If you solve my riddle during these seven days of the celebration, I will give you thirty plain linen robes and thirty fancy robes. But if you can't solve it, then you must give me thirty linen robes and thirty fancy robes.'

'All right,' they agreed, 'let's hear your riddle.' So he said, *'From the one who eats came something to eat; out of the strong came something sweet.'*

Three days later they were still trying to figure it out. On the fourth day they said to Samson's wife, 'Get the answer to the riddle from your husband, or we will burn down your father's house with you in it. Did you invite us to this party just to make us poor?' So Samson's wife came to him in tears and said, 'You don't love me; you hate me! You have given my people a riddle, but you haven't told me the answer.' 'I haven't even given the answer to my father or mother,' he replied. 'Why should I tell you?' So she cried whenever she was with him and kept it up for the rest of the celebration. **At last, on the seventh day, he told her the answer because of her persistent nagging. Then she gave the answer to the young men.**

So before sunset of the seventh day, the men of the town came to Samson with their answer: *'What is sweeter than honey? What is stronger than a lion?'*

Samson replied, 'If you hadn't plowed with my heifer, you wouldn't have found the answer to my riddle!!' Then the Spirit of the LORD powerfully took control of him. He went down to the town of Ashkelon, killed thirty men, took their belongings, and gave their clothing to the men who had answered his riddle. But Samson was furious about what had happened, and he went back home to live with his father and mother. So his wife was given in marriage to the man who had been Samson's best man at the wedding." *NLT*

It is critical to notice the progression as we see this real life drama unfold. We see these people being deceived by Samson and later we find that Samson is also deceived. It is such a good example of God teaching us this lesson straight from the pages of His book.

Judges 16:
"Samson had great strength. He was the Judge for Israel for twenty years. His attraction for women was his downfall. Delilah was another woman whom he also loved. The Philistines approached her and offered her money to betray Samson. She was to find out his source of power. He played with her and told her several different tales about where his strength came from. Each time the Philistines came in to capture him he would get out of whatever they had tried to bind him in and break free. His strength allowed him to rid himself of them. The Philistines would not give up. Delilah would not give up. Delilah had been threatened. The Philistines had

threatened to harm her family if she did not cooperate with their plot to be rid of Samson. She had been deceived by her friends; now she would deceive Samson. It is a vicious circle." *NLT*

Judges 16:17

"Samson finally told her. 'My hair has never been cut,' he confessed, 'for I was dedicated to God as a Nazarite from Birth. If my head were shaved, my strength would leave me, and I would become as weak as anyone else.'

He fell asleep in her lap and she cut his hair. The Philistines charged in and captured him. When he woke up, he thought, 'I will do as before and shake myself free.' But he didn't realize the LORD had left him." *NLT*

Judges 16:20

"But he didn't realize the LORD had left him. That is such a sad commentary of this whole event. His strength came from the Lord. His hair had been cut and he wasn't aware. He had fallen asleep." NLT

What did they do with Him?

Judges 16:21

"The Philistines gouged out his eyes. They took him to Gaza, where he was bound with bronze chains and made to grind grain in the prison. But before long his hair began to grow back." *NLT*

- **We are deceived when we have wrong desires.**

- **We are deceived when we compromise our values.**

- **We are deceived when we confuse our priorities.**

What Steps Can We Take To Avoid the Deception of Sin?

Some lessons can only be learned by experience!

I am not sure how old I was when it dawned upon me how much I liked gold. Maybe I was born with this desire for gold. It could be earrings, which I did not wear, gold rings, gold necklaces, gold anything. I was attracted to gold.

One of the girls in my neighborhood had this gold ring. It was beautiful and she assured me *it was pure gold*. That was all I needed to hear. I was fascinated by her gold ring. She told me she would *let me buy it for $2.00*. I saved and saved. Finally I bought the gold ring *for $2.00*.

Two weeks later when my finger had, along with my gold ring, turned green, I started to feel like I had been deceived. I had been deceived because I had allowed my desire for *pure gold to trap me*. My mother finally told me, "You can always tell when gold is real by looking inside of the ring or some-where on the gold necklace. It will say '10 karat gold' or '12 karat gold.'" Another wise person said, "If it sounds too good to be true, then it probably is." I learned that *real gold* is more valuable than $2.00. I also learned to "ask around." My inno-cence had been robbed and my knowledge of gold was a bit more defined. I became "street smart" about purchasing pure gold. Learning about the value of gold has been a lasting example for me.

I have heard it said that when bank tellers are being trained how to distinguish real money and phony money there is a simple truth that must prevail. They teach the tellers to know what the real money looks like and feels like. They have to learn what the real thing is first before they can point out the counterfeit. When we think we are getting something for nothing, or if the bargain is too good to believe, we had better examine it a little closer. Our greed will often allow us to be deceived.

Edna's Parables: We are deceived when our greed gets in the way and when we aren't sure of the genuine article. We settle for fool's gold.

We deceive ourselves first.

Galatians 6:7
"We deceive ourselves when we think we can get away with sin. We deceive ourselves when we think we can ignore God and still receive his blessing." *NLT*

I Corinthians 3:18
"Stop fooling yourselves. If you think you are wise by this world's standards, you will have to become a fool so you can become wise by God's standards." *NLT*

Careful! Deceitfulness in Progress...

One of the reasons we are so easily deceived is because we don't recognize it as a situation where we are going to be deceived. We are not expecting anyone to deceive us. Another area we need to be guarded in is learning to recognize that darkness may have the appearance of light. We also do not expect anyone from our church to purposefully deceive us, but it happens.

When groups of people in churches promote themselves as being the final authority regarding spiritual insight, we need to test what is being said in the light of Scripture. This kind of deception has been called by others "spiritual abuse." This is a strong statement, but even though the church family should be a safe place, we know that it isn't always safe. I am not saying that we shouldn't trust those in the church, but I am saying people can be deceived from within the walls of the church. We need to evaluate what we hear and what we see by the Word of God. People may appear to be walking in the light, but we need to take time examining whose light they are reflecting.

> **II Timothy 3:13**
> "Evil people and impostors will flourish. They will go on deceiving others, and they themselves will be deceived." *NLT*

We have taken people into our home and they have robbed us, lied to us and basically destroyed our trust. We have tried to help people over the years and they have ended up deceiving us. Sometimes it was over a period of years and sometimes it was only for a short time. We felt used by them. We felt violated, we wondered why we didn't recognize the enemy's plot sooner. We wondered why God allowed this to happen to our family. They took advantage of us and our children. We have learned from these experiences. Hopefully, they have learned as well.

When we try to cover up the truth we become the *deceitful ones*. We do not want to acknowledge that we could be the deceiver but it is possible because we are susceptible to sin. We don't always live in the power of the Holy Spirit. All we can do is confess it as sin and pray for forgiveness.

Our sinful behavior may take the form of someone who manipulates others. It may manifest itself as "one who knows to do good, but doesn't do it." This is an area that we all must guard. Remember who the *Father of Lies is: The devil himself.* His tactics are to first attack us in a weak area of our character. He sometimes uses partial truth, as it was in the garden of Eden when the serpent quoted only part of what God had said, "Thou shalt not surely die." He uses the same tactics on us and we fall as well.

1 John 1:3-10

"This is the message he has given us to announce to you: God is light and there is no darkness in him at all. So we are lying if we say we have fellowship with God, but go on living in spiritual darkness. We are not living in the truth. But if we are living in the light of God's presence, just as Christ is, then we have fellowship with each other, and the blood of Jesus, his Son, cleanses us from every sin.

If we say we have no sin, we are only fooling ourselves and refusing to accept the truth. But if we confess our sins to him, he is faithful and just to forgive us and to cleanse us from every wrong. If we claim we have not sinned, we are calling God a liar and showing that his word has no place in our hearts." *NLT*

As believers, we need to <u>guard our hearts</u> in whatever area we are facing temptation. We have to examine our hearts to see what is really happening. Being aware of our motives is a good clue for helping us in this area. We are conscious of those areas because the Holy Spirit reveals them to us. Sometimes we are naive. Our friends can also help us identify the blind spots we cannot see for ourselves. When we take the risk to ask for help, God will provide the information we need to make better choices. We can also ask our friends.

They will be able to point out areas we simply do not see.

Guard Your Hearts!

- In relationships
- At our workplace
- In business dealings
- As spiritual leaders

In any area where integrity is needed.

Set your heart on the things above...not on the things that have the center stage of this world. It can creep up on you and you hardly take notice.

I was visiting with one of my sons and we were having a conversation about the influence of television. It has moved into our living rooms, our bedrooms, our playrooms. It is in every part of our homes. We were discussing our reactions to the first time we heard swear words on television. It was an easy choice. I just got up and turned it off. We didn't have remote control. We are not gross sinners because we watch television, we have just become conditioned to what we are watching. We have become desensitized to what is going on in our own living rooms. We can deceive ourselves. This is very hard to admit.

We need to **check our motives**. Why am I doing this? How does this bring glory to Christ? If I continue on this path, where will this lead me five minutes from now?

I remember the tale of a man who lived in the East. This man spent his time traveling around the country selling his wares. His culture was very different from ours. He cared for his camels but his life was lonely. He had his simple life and his simple routine. Each night he would feed and bed down his camels and then eat his simple meal by the fire. He would then retire for the evening in his tent.

One night a camel put his nose inside the tent, and the old man thought to himself, "OH WELL." The next day they traveled a long distance and the same procedure for the evening took place. Except this evening the camel came in a little further and the old traveler allowed him to stay. It was cold and what harm could come from it? It was company for the old man.

This continued on....until the camel was sleeping inside the tent and the old man was sleeping outside in the cold. He was out in the cold in the dessert, without the warmth of his tent. He lost his position in the tent. Deception is subtle. GUARD YOUR HEART.

Deception Enslaves

When we come to know Christ, we come to know the truth. Christ came to set us free not to place us in bondage or under a curse. We know the truth but at times we do not apply it to our daily lives. The devil is a master at deceiving us. We must recognize his tricks and stand against his footholds.

His tricks have names: **Deception, Distrust, Disruption, Dissension, Doubt, Discouragement, Depression, Daydreaming, Dollars, and Dessert**.

The truth will not lead you to be enslaved to this world and its devices. The entrapments of guilt, addictions and whatever else you might think of will continue to rule your life. There is not always freedom in doing your *own thing*. Secular thinking will say, do it your way, be your own person, follow your dreams, but they never show us where all of this can finally end. This is not freedom! We are not in control when we are living in sin. We are being controlled. We cannot break out of the bondage unless we learn how to walk in the Spirit. When the devil is in control, we are not living in the truth.

When we know the truth, the truth will set us free.

When we give our hearts to the Lord, our desire will be for how we can serve him. We have a new purpose. A strong desire for all of us is to have our own way. We get involved with a power struggle and we are often **motivated by power** when making our choices. We have nothing within ourselves that can free us from the bondage of sin and its control over our lives. We are powerless without the presence of the Holy Spirit working in our lives.

Galatians 5:1
"So Christ has really set us free. Now make sure that you stay free, and don't get tied up again in slavery to the law." *NLT*

People are addicted to all kinds of things these days. **Power** is one of the things that people become addicted to. They want to be in charge, they want to be able to handle their problems by themselves. Money, when used in the wrong way, will also help complete the vicious circle of being a slave to deception. Nothing outside of Christ can bring **true happiness**. We must not allow ourselves to be deceived by what appears to be successful, or what might bring some short-term happiness. It cannot last.

Romans 7:5-6
"When we were controlled by our old nature, sinful desires were at work within us, and the law aroused these evil desires that produced sinful deeds, resulting in death. But now we have been released from the

law, for we died with Christ, and we are no longer captive to its power. Now we can really serve God, not in the old way by obeying the letter of the law, but in the new way, by the Spirit." *NLT*

Consider This:

This is the bottom line. When you realize you are deceiving or being deceived, confess your sin and ask for forgiveness. Ask the Lord for discernment. Ask the Lord to help you, and then move on. It takes courage to admit your mistakes and your part in being deceived. Process your motives. Why did I get so easily caught up in that? Sometimes it is so obvious, other times it is subtle. Ask another person to help you in the area of your life where your thinking doesn't fit with God's Word.

_____

_____

_____

_____

_____

_____

Chapter Eight

CAMPING OUT

I must confess that camping is one of my favorite past-times. We used to camp as a family. In fact, at one place where we lived we made a camping spot right on our property. It was by our spring, and we made a place to build a fire and to cook. When we couldn't get away for some camping time we would go out in the back of our house and we would camp. Sometimes in the middle of the day. I would call the boys and we go together to our camping spot for lunch. It was a quick getaway and a time of refreshment.

Some of our friends enjoyed camping as well. When they came over we would head for the camp site to cook our food in the camping area. The kids would play in the trees that provided the shade for our site. Those were special times for our family.

After the meal, we would burn the paper plates and build up the fire. We would sometimes sing around the camp fire or just visit until the mosquitoes came along and we had to cut short our time at the camp site. We could always go up to the house, but the atmosphere seemed to be lost in the transition to the house.

It was close by, we could carry our stuff back to the house, we could have the kids take their baths and they could sleep in their own beds. No tent had to be put up. We didn't have to worry about the trash. The kitchen didn't have to be swept. It was a wonderful place for our family outings. The absence of travel time was also a major factor in helping us manage our time.

When we moved to Minnesota, we discovered that camping was a really big thing up there. People camped and had cabins and the woods were everywhere. People took whole vacations and camped. They went on their honeymoons and camped! I did think that was a bit quaint, but the people were into camping. They were enthusiastic campers. They had great stories to tell and it was part of their lives. They even camped in the middle of winter.

Bill got caught up in this camping idea as well. We celebrated our anniversary one year on January 30th at a friend's cabin. We had to leave the car by the road and walk to the cabin with our camping gear. We carried in our sleeping bags, food, water, and an electric heater. The snow was up to my thighs and I could barely walk up the lane to the cabin.

Bill kept calling back words of encouragement. "Isn't this great? We are out here, no phones, no one to bother us. Isn't this just perfect?" I am sure our friends, the Swanstroms, thought we were totally crazy. They had allowed us to use their cabin. We were camping out in 30 degree below zero weather, and that was not the wind chill. People do such crazy things, all for the sake of love and romance, and call it camping. How sentimental can you get?

We did crazy things as it related to camping, but so did some of the other folks that lived in Minnesota. Camping was a very popular topic. One night we were to go to our friend's house for our small group meeting. She was a busy person with lots of things going on in her life. She was a single parent and had a lot of responsibilities. When we arrived at her home...it was the best comic relief we had ever experienced, bar none, as it related to small group experience. Margaret had her whole living room set up like a camping site. I am serious! The clothesline with hanging towels struck me first. I am not sure if it was truly laundry drying or not. I would not have put this past creative Margaret. Huge logs to sit on...a fire...but I can't remember if it was in the fireplace or if it was a fake one. We ate hot dogs and camp food. It was a stitch. The tent was set up in the living room as well. Blankets were hanging around, draped over the furniture. It was a camp site.

Margaret was a clever gal, she hadn't had time to clean her house and worry about how everything looked. We were coming and we were her small group and she made it a wonderful memory and a wonderful time. We get so caught up in living out our lives here on this earth that we often forget that we are really **camping out**!

While on staff with Inter-Varsity Christian Fellowship, Bill and I spent a couple of months living at Mackinac Island. It is a beautiful place and it was another one of those once-in-a-life-time experiences. Bill and I fell in love with the island the moment we stepped off of the ferry boat. There were no cars or motor vehicles of any kind except for the fire engine that no one saw unless it was needed. For us, Mackinac Island was something of a romantic getaway.

IVCF is a ministry geared for working with students on the campus as well as outreach ministries in this country and around the world. Our job was to build a team of students that would be strong in their faith. They would in turn get to know the students working on the island and eventually have the opportunity to share Christ with their newly made friends. It is called Friendship Evangelism.

Students just like themselves who had acquired jobs for the summer in the local shops and restaurants were the focus of the ministry. This was truly a mission field. In all, some 1,800 students were there from all parts of the United States. These IVCF students worked harder than any students I have ever met. Of course the purpose of their earnings was for their college tuition even if this was a vacation site. They were very energetic and enthusiastic, and clearly loved Jesus. It was a good experience for them. In later years they have often told us how this time influenced them for a deeper commitment to Christ as well as the vocational choices they made.

But this was a secular world and it could be a hard place to be a Christian. It was a place where your faith was tested on every turn. In fact, drugs were plentiful, as was drinking and sexual compromise. We called this place "Sin Island." Mackinac Island by appearance was definitely a beautiful place to spend a holiday. To see its historical attractions was like stepping back in time. And yet the corruption of our modern world was always coming to the surface. This is why it was a mission field of wasted and needy young people.

It was easy to see that the island's population was composed of several different groups of people. Naturally, there were the year round residents known as <u>the town people</u>. I am sure when the summer was over they enjoyed their quiet village again as they reclaimed their homes and community. Some of them rented out their homes during the vacation season, so it was also economically very profitable for them.

<u>The students</u> described earlier were there for the summer to work in the shops and restaurants and to have fun at it. And their presence clearly represented a distinct people group.

But their purpose was really to serve another group, affectionately known as <u>the fudgies</u>. This was the name given to the tourists. They were given this name by all of us who were there for more than a day visit. You could recognize the fudgies because they carried their plastic bags with their fudge from the different fudge shops. After you were there for a while you knew the best fudge from the "other fudge". You knew it by the taste and texture. The fudgies wanted to buy good fudge but would not have our advantage. They could not tell the difference until they bought fudge from several shops. If you lived there you didn't waste time shopping and only bought it from your favorite shop. But it was like an addiction.

There was also a small population which represented the <u>Indian community</u>. They lived in the center of the island, away from all the tourist. Bill developed a special interest in this group as well.

There were also some special town people who didn't have to rent their residences out. Many of these folks lived on the island's hill with the best views and were known as <u>The richies</u>.

We also recognized the <u>Shop owners</u> as a distinct group. It was a great mix of people. It may seem silly now, but everyone had a name and were identified in this manner during conversations. We were probably called <u>The religious</u> people by them. Some of us have maintained relationships to this day. We keep thinking we should have some sort of reunion but I don't know how we would get in touch with all of them. Serving the Lord brings us into contact with so many delightful people. It is one of the benefits of being in ministry.

But true to our purpose, we felt most connected to the vast number of students there, not just the IVCF plants who became family to us. This mission field of student may have been without a clue as to what our mission experience was about. But in the kingdom view, they were there because God had called them for such a time as this. Our love for them in Christ is what connected us to them . Our team all worked to bring many into the family of Christ. It was not like any ministry I had ever experienced. IVCF served God in a very special way during this time. Bill and I learned many things while working with the fudgies and the students. It was a timeless experience and is a great memory.

1 Peter 1:13-25

"Therefore, prepare your minds for action: be self controlled; set your hope fully on the grace to be given you when Jesus Christ is revealed. As obedient children, do not conform to the evil desires you had when you lived in ignorance. But just as he who called you is holy, so be holy in all you do; for it is written: "Be holy, because I am holy. Since you call on a Father who judges each man's work impartially, live your lives as **strangers** here in reverent fear."
NLT

I think the Lord is calling us all to be like <u>the fudgies</u> but to minister like <u>the students</u> who ministered as strangers in reverent fear, holy and set apart. We aren't supposed to get too attached to this world and its cares and concerns.

> "For you know that it was not with perishable things such as silver or gold that you were redeemed from the empty way of life handed down to you from your forefathers, but with the precious blood of Christ, a lamb without blemish or defect. He was chosen before the creation of the world, but was revealed in these last times for your sake. Through him you believe in God, who raised him from the dead and glorified him, and so your faith and hope are in God.

> Now that you have purified yourselves be obeying the truth so that you have sincere love for your brothers, love one another deeply, from the heart. For you have been born again, not of perishable seed, but of imperishable, through the living and enduring word of God. For, 'All men are like grass, and all their glory is like the flowers of the field; the grass withers and the flowers fall, but the word of the Lord stands forever.' And this is the word that was preached to you." *NLT*

Student / Tourist Information:

1.   Keep the lines moving.

Prepare your minds for ACTION. Be self controlled, set your hope fully on the grace that has been given to you, as you wait for Christ's return.

2.   Obey the signs, like "Don't touch the POISON IVY!"

As obedient children...don't conform to what is going on around you. Do not be partakers of the corruption that is all around us. Be holy!

3. Be prepared to leave when the bus driver honks the horn!

Remember we are **Camping Out**, we are tourists. Sometimes while we are camping we get too attached to the camp site. We would like to make the camp site our home. We are here temporarily. Our surroundings should not be the focus for our lives. We have to ask the Lord to help us deal with setting the right priorities. We have to count the cost and discipline ourselves not to value the things of this world more than our relationship with God.

4. Be a good representative of your home and family name.

Remember, we are to be witnesses and we are to live as forgiven people so others can learn of him. This is just our earthly home and we are passing through, waiting until He comes again.

5. Bathe regularly and often.

While we are camping we often do not have access to a bath. Isn't is good to get home and take a good tub bath? While we are passing through we get corrupted by the lust of the eyes, the pride of life. We buy into secular thinking and it leaves its mark upon us. We have to constantly claim the blood of Christ for cleansing. We have to avoid the deception that is all around us.

6. Be kind to the natives and the environment. Take out what you bring in.

Learn to accept and love one another. We need to observe the rules at the camp site. We need to learn once again to respect others and the cultural environment in which we are placed to minister. I guess we have to collect our trash from time to time, and sometimes we have to pick up after others as well.

When we went to Mackinac Island, it was very difficult to leave. We left the students to finish out the summer and we had to return to Minnesota. It was good for us to leave them in order for them to learn to apply what they had learned. It gave them the chance to develop their leadership skills and sharpen their wits while learning to rely upon the Lord. We often have to remind ourselves of our purpose for being left here on this earth.

Where Your Treasure is, There your Heart will be also.

Matthew. 6:19-22
"Do not store up for yourselves treasures on earth, where moth and rust destroy, and where thieves break in and steal. But store up for yourselves treasures in heaven, where moth and rust do not destroy, and where thieves do not break in and steal. For where your treasure is, there your heart will be also." *NLT*

This last move caused me to realize some things about myself. I had a lot of junk in my life. I know I keep calling them antiques but mostly it is junk and stuff. I think I carried most of it around because it somehow gave me a sense of security. But I had to move beyond finding comfort from things. I had to find my security not in where I am but Who I am with. When I rely upon the Lord, his peace will surround me. I am finally starting to grasp the truth of what it means to **just camp out**. We're just passing through.

Maybe this is how God prepares our hearts for heaven. The

things around us have to be viewed with different eyes. Our eyes need a new vision, the true vision. We may need to ask God to give us His view of our world.

Spiritual Eye Examination, Conducted Here!

Matthew 6:22-24
"The eye is the lamp of the body. If your eyes are good, your whole body will be full of light. But if your eyes are bad, your whole body will be full of darkness. If then the light within you is darkness, how great is that darkness!" *NLT*

Hopefully, we are starting to look at this concept of camping out as Christ would have us view it. Things and life are temporal. The only thing that really matters is knowing where to place our hope. We need to allow God to control our focus. We cannot teach others what we ourselves have not experienced.

As we get older our physical eyesight gets weaker. We begin to need additional help in seeing. But I pray that my spiritual eyes are finally in focus with what God is trying to teach me. I want to have the eyes and mind of Christ in what I do and what I say. Could it be that I am "FINALLY GETTING IT!"

How long will it take before you finally just OBEY?

The children of Israel spent a lot of time **camping out**. They wandered around for 40 years looking for their home. They didn't take the direct route. They seemed to be lost and constantly concerned with the scenic route. A whole generation had to pass away because they were not ready to obey God. They wanted to do it their way, and on their terms. They became comfortable with what had rubbed off on them from their stay in Egypt. They had picked up some of the ways and values of the Egyptians. They had forgotten their first love for

God. They kept remembering the leeks and the garlic. They seemed to have forgotten the bondage and the making of bricks without straw. How quickly we forget. It seems we all deal with selective hearing, selective vision and selective memory.

We may be wondering at this point, What traits have we gathered from the lives of those around us? Our world is polluted because we have polluted it. We are the guilty ones. We cannot blame this on past generations. We must assume responsibility for our own decisions. **"We can choose, we can change, we can risk, and we can fail"** - sometimes not in that order, and sometimes all within one hour of the same day.

Obedience seems too demanding. Does God really demand that we obey Him completely? God's law is exacting. God does have a plan and a purpose for our lives. *Be holy, even as I am holy.* He is God and He can do whatever He wants. He is God, and we are the ones He created. He is the potter, we are the clay. He is in charge of your shift and mine.

Deuteronomy 6:25
"Do what is right and good in the LORD's sight, so all will go well with you." *NLT*

It doesn't appear to me that God is calling upon us for a vote. Moses did not fully obey and trust God in the desert experience and that is why he was not allowed to go into the promised land. He was allowed to see it, but not to go into the land.

Numbers 20:1-13
"God said to Moses, "Because you did not trust me enough...you will not lead them into the land." *NLT*

Disobedience for all of us, as well as for the spiritual leaders of our day, has its fall-out. When we fail to obey we do not do

135

well. God allows us grace and mercy, but He also expects us to OBEY.

Some people think that if they obey the Ten Commandments they will be able to satisfy the justice of God and thereby enter into Heaven. But there is none who are able to obey the Law. What we must do is plead the mercy of God by confessing our sin, and accepting the provision of what Jesus did on the cross. The way of the cross leads home. We are not to set up a permanent residence. We are **camping out**. We will not be able to enjoy the reward of Heaven unless we accept the gift of salvation. The gift of salvation is God's gift of "His SON." Our obedience in accepting His
provision for us shows our expression of love and thankfulness for what Christ did on the cross. He paid for our sins. We show Him respect when we obey. When we choose not to obey, we sin. "Without Him we can do nothing."

Obedience brings it's own set of rewards....everlasting life, for one. Christ said the only way we could come to the Father was through accepting Him. If we choose not to obey His call upon our lives, we will miss out on eternity.

> **Jeremiah. 7:23**
> "This is what I told them: Obey me, and I will be your God, and you will be my people. Only do as I say, and all will be well!" *NLT*

Moses and the children of Israel spent a long time **camping out** because of disobedience. It was 40 years in the wilderness. It could have been a lot shorter journey. We see this when we look at the map of the area. The path of obedience seems a lot shorter than the path of rebellion they chose.

John 14:6

"Jesus told him, "I am the Way, the Truth, and the Life. No one can come to the Father except through me." *NLT*

If we do not obey what Jesus said in regard to going to Heaven, we will never enter the promised land. We will spend eternity in hell...and I don't think the camp site there is one anyone would enjoy. I encourage you to "Come and go with me to my father's house." I know the Way and I will help you to take down your tent and to prepare for your permanent dwelling place - the place that Jesus is now preparing for you and for me. "I go to prepare a place for you, and where I am, there you will be too."

Consider This:

Have you looked at your camp site lately? Has it become so comfortable that you have forgotten that soon you will need to head for your home? What has replaced your first love? Have you become attached to something, someone, or some career, maybe even some ministry, more than your relationship with God? Do you think about eternity and the second coming of Christ? Do you believe that Jesus is coming again?

_____

_____

_____

_____

_____

Chapter Nine

COUNT YOUR BLESSINGS!

It doesn't matter what you have been through in the past, or what you may be going through now; there has to be something positive in your life.

Spending time with people who have experienced depression has made one thing very clear to me. There are many different ways people deal with depression. A common finding is that depression attacks us when we are most vulnerable. It may be during periods of bad health or a side-effect of medication. One of the first questions I ask my friends when they seem to be dealing with depression is when they last had a complete physical.

The feelings of depression may not be easy to describe or understand. We can feel out of touch with our surroundings and those we know and love. We have feelings of guilt and despair. We may feel invisible. Sometimes we isolate ourselves from others and then wonder why no one has noticed we are missing. We can all experience depression to some degree. This is not a choice we make, to be depressed. It doesn't really matter what event or circumstance has brought us to this place. The point is, we are depressed.

I also know that it is hard for us to think in terms of thankfulness and praise when we are dealing with deep depression. We have forgotten how to count our blessings because we are so overwhelmed by our problems. And sometimes we experience depression when we are failing to cope with the losses in our lives. I find that if we can just offer up one thing that we can be thankful for, or one thought on how we can praise God, we can eventually build personal hope again. It is a choice to be well. We have to focus on God, and ask for His help in our healing process.

During times of depression, He can still reveal His will to us. As we are seeking Him, He may reveal to us the next step. He sent the raven to feed Elijah when he was depressed and lonely. God is not limited in His ways of sending us help and encouragement. His help may come in the form of simply giving us the courage to tell someone our feelings. He gives spurts of energy and strength when ours has been drained. The God who provides is still alive and available to us today. Our God is still able!

Thankfulness and praise defuse the enemy's foothold in dealing with the battle of depression!

Many things can trigger depression: a perceived injustice, or a feeling of utter helplessness. Sometimes it is just carrying more responsibility than we have the energy to handle. Sometimes it is necessary to restructure our lifestyles to get rid of some of our stress. We can get weighed down with worry. Frustration and feelings of despair are common emotions people deal with when they are suffering from depression. As mentioned before, medical causes exist. There may be a hidden chemical imbalance within our body that is actually causing some of the symptoms. Even when we make the effort to get help or we are given medication for our depression it may take time to experience wholeness and health. The progress can be slow.

Christians do have to live with depression, too. There are many causes and none of us are exempt. We may be relationally "in Christ" and still experience depression. God doesn't condemn us because we are depressed. He wants to walk beside us through this time in life. The Lord is not going to judge us for having experienced depression. David was a man after God's own heart and it is evident in his writings, the Psalms, that he was sometimes depressed. We can know the Lord in a very deep way and live with depression.

But denial is not the answer. When we are down, and hide the fact from our friends, we end up adding more anxiety to our depression. We may be fearful of what others will think. But we must admit it to ourselves and take the responsibity to get help. I have had conversations with friends who were afraid to share this about themselves for fear they would be judged too harshly or labeled. But this does not allow the body of Christ to come along side and bear one anther's burdens. It is true some would judge us, and that is a risk. But we should not try to carry this burden alone.

I lived with my husband Bill for thirty-nine years, plus. He lived and dealt with depression for some of that time. It would sometimes come over him for no apparent reason. He would be quiet and withdrawn. Sometimes, he would just say, "I'm feeling lonely today." I took that as a signal to let him know that, first of all, I would pray for him, and I would be available if he wanted to talk.

Depression can come from feelings of guilt. It is important to keep short books with God. Bill was a person very much in touch with his feelings and often would compose poetry or write in his journal. His writings helped him openly admit that he was not doing very well that day. His depression could last for weeks and months at a time. It was difficult for both of us. He had a sweet spirit and he loved life. But he was often depressed.

Naturally, his medical conditions contributed. He was a diabetic, and he was asthmatic. A part of his depression was caused by some of the medication he took on a daily basis as prescribed by his doctors. His physical limitations put restrictions upon him, and after years of living with his physical problems it took its toll on his emotions as well. He did not enjoy taking two shots of insulin daily, and 57 pills every day. Those medications were for maintenance and for helping him feel as well as he did. He did not complain and he was a true fighter but there were times when I am sure he felt overwhelmed.

Bill's journalizing was therapeutic for him and a safe place to express his emotions. It helps to write thoughts and feelings. It gives us an opportunity to let out those emotions we tend to stuff. It is good to look at them on paper, in black and white. It is also good to talk to someone about our feelings as well. Counseling can be very helpful in dealing with depression. Some negative ways we deal with depression are overeating, smoking, drinking, gambling. sleep disorders and other

142

forms of escape. Isolating ourselves from others may be a coping mechanism because it is too hard to share the feelings.

All of the creative things he did were for him a healthy choice for coping with feelings. Now when I read some of the things he wrote in his journal it is clear how God took him through those times and brought him over to the other side. Those pages and pages of his journal minister to me now, helping me to cope with my loss. It helps me to see the faithfulness of God to Bill during this time. Bill's faith and love for God were evident even in his depression. We need to be faithful in trying to reach out to others during their depression.

David of the Old Testament wrote about his depression many times.

He refers to his need for God.

Psalm 119:80-84
"May I be blameless in keeping your principles; then I will never have to be ashamed. I faint with longing for your salvation; but I have put my hope in your word. My eyes are straining to see your promises come true. When will you comfort me? I am shriveled like a wineskin in the smoke, exhausted with waiting. But I cling to your principles and obey them. How long must I wait?" *NLT*

In this passage, we see David's dispair. His life is open for all to see. He feels so desperate. He continues expressing his feelings and he starts to direct his thoughts to the Lord for help.

Psalm 119:114
"You are my refuge and my shield; your word is my only source of hope." *NLT*

When we rely on the word as a source of help, we will be helped. His promises are always true.

I am not saying that I do not believe Christians should take medication for depression. *I am not saying* that I think anyone is less spiritual if they need to seek counsel as they plow through some of their pain. I am saying that God will direct you through wise counseling and through His Word. Many people rely upon the Word, medication, and wise counseling as they find hope and recovery.

Our attitude in offering praise and thanksgiving will help us through difficult times. It may not solve all of our depression, but it allows us to know that something in our lives is positive. God wants to assure us of His love and He wants to give us hope.

In the New Testament, Paul gives us a little excerpt from what his life was about as a missionary in his letter to the Church at Corinth.

II Corinthians 1:3-11
"All praise to the God and Father of our Lord Jesus Christ. He is the source of every mercy and the God who comforts us. He comforts us in all our troubles so that we can comfort others. When others are troubled, we will be able to give them the same comfort God has given us. You can be sure that the more we suffer for Christ, the more God will shower us with his comfort through Christ. So when we are **weighed down with troubles**, it is for your benefit and salvation! For when God comforts us, it is so that we, in turn, can be an encouragement to you. Then you can patiently endure the same things we suffer. We are confident that as you share in suffering, you will also share God's comfort.

I think you ought to know, dear friends, about the trouble we went through in the province of Asia. We were crushed and completely overwhelmed, and we thought we could never live through it. In fact, we expected to die. But as a result, we learned NOT TO RELY ON OURSELVES, but on God who can raise the dead. And he did deliver us from mortal danger. And we are confident that he will continue to deliver us. He will rescue us because you are helping by praying for us. As a result, many will give thanks to God because so many people's prayers for our safety have been answered." *NLT*

We can learn from Paul's words.

- He offers praise to God. Count your blessings!
- Paul had total trust in God's Word and His promises.
- Do not rely upon yourself for the answers. You are not the resource.
- Ask others to pray for you and pray yourself.
- Expect God to use your situation in your life to help others when they face similar trials.
- Because of your circumstances, God will help you to be sensitive to the needs of others.
- Count your Blessings as you suffer for Christ.

These phrases sound like what one of my friends called speaking in "Christianese". Familiar terms, but how do they become practical in the real world? We can't just say to others, Count your blessings and forget your pain. We have to walk with them and listen as they share their grief. The body of Christ needs to take an active part in helping others live through their pain. It takes time and energy to be part of the healing process.

It often comes down to the question of asking ourselves, will God be enough? God is the source of all the help we need. He sends us the answers and if He doesn't, He promises to be with us during the storm. Sometimes we feel worse before it gets better.

Along with Paul, I have found His grace to be sufficient. We experience difficulties and we experience grief and loss. Some of us have been close to death, but in spite of the hardships, we can count on the faithfulness of God. We know the blessings of God in our lives but often we neglect our expressions of thankfulness. We can get beyond the pain if we allow the Healer to come to our rescue. It may surprise us how the Lord ministers to us through the valleys.

The media, our educational system and the self help crowd are often heard offering a similar message. That message is that we have a supreme power within ourselves for healing, for success and to overcome depression. Whatever we desire can be found if we look within ourselves. But we are not the center of anything. We are the creation, not the Creator. His grace is sufficient for our need. When it has traveled the full circle, our desperation will eventually bring us face to face with our inadequacy. The only way out of this circle is to completely trust in God's character.

The Blessing of knowing Him as Lord.

God takes us through the valleys and mountain top experiences to teach us about His faithfulness. When experiencing these times in our lives it is important to remember that we will find no water at the **top of those mountains**.

We were traveling across the dry and desolate mountains in southern Arizona on our way to California. It was hot, and we were drinking our bottled water, not to be trendy, but because our thirst needed to be quenched. We noticed as we traveled through these mountains, there was no water or vegetation. It was barren. The water could be found in the valleys. Yes, in the valleys they used irrigation but the water was still in the valleys. There wasn't any water on top of the mountains.

God takes us through deep things to complete his work in our hearts. When we are learning the lessons of suffering we are also learning the lessons of comfort. When we accepted Christ we also accepted the suffering along with the blessings. God promises to be with us in the dry times as well as the times of plenty.

His Lordship in our lives confronts our distorted thinking..

What is held dearest to our hearts is eventually what must be given to the Lord. Relationships, false security derived from our material junk, self esteem, all must be given over to Him. This is a struggle because we do not want to give up anything. We want to take the camp site home. It is desirable to be in control of whatever is going on in our lives. We struggle to limit pride, self reliance and control issues. It is a continual battle to just lay it all down and let go of whatever hinders us from walking in complete fellowship with Him. Responding to His Lordship brings fellowship and right thinking.

Count Your Blessings while you wait.

When we are waiting on God it can be hard to believe that He cares, or to count blessings. It is even harder to trust God for the lives of those you love. You may be able to believe in the promises of God for yourself but it is hard to believe that they also apply to those you love. Especially if it seems to you they have lost interest in God.

It seemed to us for a time that Michael, our oldest son, was not interested in God or aware of his need for Him in his life. I was afraid for him because I knew he had trusted Christ for his salvation but he was not in fellowship with Him. I could not even talk about it with him. I knew that something in his life was tearing him apart. He was running from the Lord and going nowhere.

He had suffered a severe injury to his wrist and it had taken months and months to heal. Finally, he had surgery again, which was another traumatic experience. When we are young we usually heal quickly, but his arm was not cooperating. And the young are not the best at being patient. But Michael was experiencing the hand of God, and it wasn't a pleasant time for him or for us. It was hard to see this as a blessing of God upon his life.

I wanted God to stop the pain. I wanted God to quickly heal Michael's arm. I was trying to interpret God's will for Michael based upon my own comfort zone. It was many years later before I realized that God was teaching Michael about patience and dependence upon Him. God was teaching Michael about being Lord of his life and it had nothing to do with me or his father. Michael was learning what God was teaching him. Michael had been dealing with depression over this injury to his arm, it had affected his whole life. Now I can clearly see it was part of God's plan for Michael to teach him more about Himself. He needed to establish his own faith in God. He needed to learn how to depend upon God's word for himself, but in the meantime, I was going to give him some counsel on "God's will for His life, by way of his mother."

One day while he was shaving I was standing in the doorway trying to talk with him about his relationship with the Lord. Parents are very good at talking to their children about God's will for their lives. I had a captive audience and I wanted to jump in and help God out with this problem. Like God wasn't aware, or that God needed my help.

While he was shaving he was listening but then he turned to me and said, "Mom, can't you trust God for me?" With his simple question, Michael encouraged me to allow God to deal directly with him. That is when I finally got the message. **I had to let it go.** I had to rely upon God, too. I could not manipulate the situation or change the path God was giving to Michael. It is almost impossible to wait upon God when you are anxious.

He went through more difficult times. He will tell you himself that the things that distracted him were real battles. I wanted so desperately to bear his pain and correct his course. Yes, he made poor choices, but in spite of it all, God was always mindful of Michael. God knows our choices and is caring for us. We must trust His Word when he says, "I will never leave you or forsake you." Michael was in God's hands, not mine.

Michael still had to go through other deep valleys in his life. He experienced the pain of a broken marriage. He has witnessed the loss of several of his friends to an early death. But I know today that it was those real life happenings that allowed Michael to experience God for himself. That period in his life has helped make him the man he is today. Michael developed his own relationship with Christ and he knows **who he is in Christ**.

The Lord uses Mike now to care for his friends when they are in trouble. His friends know that he really does understand what they are feeling. He and his wife, Glenda can come along side of others when they are experiencing marital problems, drinking problems, bouts of depression. They can say to them....God will get you through it! We will pray for you. He is real with them and they are drawn to him and his relationship with Christ. "Comfort others, as we ourselves have been comforted."

We can express concern for others, even demonstrate real compassion for people in pain. We can pray for them, but until we have lived through some of the life experiences God has used to refine them we cannot relate to their pain. Your experiences may be preparing you for a ministry of care giving. Count your blessings!

My search for water has been my path. My children have their own path and their own relationship with God. They have come to know God based upon their choices. Living on the mountain top or in the valley must eventually bring us to the end of ourselves. We may be in the midst of a dry time. Seek the water of life. We may be viewing God from the mountain. It is not for us to always understand immediately what God is teaching us. Hopefully, we will be learning more of the faithfulness of God through our life experiences. We may learn about experiencing the presence of God on a weekend retreat, but we do not know how it applies to the rest of our lives until have the gift of time to live it.

The Difficult Times Have a Purpose.

When God takes our children through difficult times, we have to learn to stand aside and allow the Holy Spirit to do his work. We cannot change the events that come into the lives of those we love. There is no quick fix to our pain, depression or loss. God works in the midst of our discomfort to teach us about His comfort. The process is not cut and dried. God has a personal relationship with each of us and He does care about us and what we care about. His promises are true.

from II Corinthians 12: 1-10

Paul had been given visions and experienced an out of the body time when the Lord revealed many truths to him. But along with these great experiences he also had a thorn in the flesh, a messenger from Satan to torment him. Some say it could have been an eye disease, but Paul says it was given to him to keep him from getting proud.

> "Three different times I begged the Lord to take it away. Each time he said, 'My gracious favor is all you need. My power works best in your weakness.' So now I am glad to boast about my weaknesses, so that the power of Christ may work through me. Since I know it is all for Christ's good, I am quite content with my weaknesses and insults, hardships, persecutions, and calamities. For when I am weak, then I am strong." *NLT*

The Christian life experience includes depression, divorce, loss of loved ones, difficult times, financial losses. But God's provision for our pain is in the midst of it all. He cares for us! He knows our situations! The horrible things we are called upon to bear have a purpose. It is so hard to **count your blessings** when we feel like our lives are falling apart. The only thing we can count on for sure is God's character. **He is faithful to His Word, and He is faithful to His people**.

It isn't popular to talk about our weaknesses. We do whatever it takes to appear fearless. If our marriages are in trouble we conceal the truth as long as possible. We cover and we hide. We are still playing the game of Hide and Seek, the game played by Adam and Eve. We want to pretend that the blessings of God are upon us because our lives seem perfect, when in truth, God's blessings are always with us in the midst of the trials. God's love continues to be available to us for all our times; His love is unconditional.

When we are waiting for that miracle and it doesn't happen, we can yell and scream and honestly say to him, "I hate this!" He will be there. I wanted God to heal Bill, but it didn't happen in Milwaukee. He accepted me in the midst of my anger. My frailty was so apparent. I wanted a blessing and ignored the purpose of God. There are many ways to play Hide and Seek.

II Corinthians 13:4-9

"Although he died on the cross in weakness, he now lives by the mighty power of God. We, too, are weak, but we live in him and have God's power—the power we use in dealing with you. Examine yourselves to see if your faith is really genuine. Test yourselves. If you cannot tell that Jesus Christ is among you, it means you have failed the test. I hope you recognize that we have passed the test and are approved by God. We pray to God that you will not do anything wrong. We pray this, not to show that our ministry to you has been successful, but because we want you to do right even if we ourselves seem to have failed. Our responsibility is never to oppose the truth, but to stand for the truth at all times. We are glad to be weak, if you are really strong. What we pray for is your restoration to maturity." *NLT*

Sometimes the Great Physician's prescription of **counting your blessings** is like a time-release capsule composed of blessings along with sufferings. Grace, blessing, and suffering don't always occur for us at the same time. The blessings are released one at a time, and dosages of suffering are as well. God gives us time to digest what He is trying to do in us and through us one day, one hour, at a time with His grace. He does allow us time to experience some of the suffering as we live out our lives here on this earth. We are then able to experience His power and healing, His continued blessing.

Here are some unwanted time-released dosages of suffering:

- Times when we do not feel prepared for events in our lives.
- Times when we take on more than we need to take on.
- Times when we deliberately choose to sin.
- Times when a difficult course must be taken in order to experience future blessings.
- Times when an open stand for Christ opens us up to ridicule.
- Times when the choices others make effect our lives.

The key to dealing with suffering is staying close to God in the midst of it all.

Psalm 22:24
"For he has not ignored the suffering of the needy. He has not turned and walked away. He has listened to their cries for help." *NLT*

Psalm 126:5-6

"Those who plant in tears will harvest with shouts of joy. They weep as they go to plant their seed, but they sing as they return with the harvest." *NLT*

Lamentations 3:32-33

"Though he brings grief, he also shows compassion according to the greatness of his unfailing love. For he does not enjoy hurting people or causing them sorrow." *NLT*

Hebrews 2:18

"Since he himself has gone through suffering and temptation, he is able to help us when we are being tempted." *NLT*

I Corinthians 12:26

"If one part suffers, all parts suffer with it, and if one part is honored, all the parts are glad." *NLT*

Again, the Great Physician offers healing for our suffering. God wants to demonstrate to us His mercy when we are suffering. God offers us comfort. God does not want to see His children suffer but at times we are disciplined by our suffering. This discipline is given graciously, bathed in love.

I Peter 4:19

"So if you are suffering according to God's will, keep on doing what is right, and trust yourself to the God who made you, for he will never fail you." *NLT*

Jesus suffered on the cross in order to forgive our sins and to heal our wounds. His willingness to die on the Cross was in obedience to the Father. It is the ultimate example of his obedience to the Heavenly Father.

When our faith has been tested, our endurance grows. When our endurance is strong then we are ready to experience the blessings.

II Timothy 3:12
"Yes, and everyone who wants to live a godly life in Christ Jesus will suffer persecution." *NLT*

We will suffer because of **who we are in Christ**.

Consider This:

Can any good come from suffering? Why aren't the blessings flowing all the time? Where is that blessing when you need it?! Am I drawing near to God through this difficult time or am I complaining and whining? Don't I have any rights? How can a chapter that is called "Count Your Blessings" be so focused on depression and suffering?

Today, what hard thing in your life do you need to share with another person, so they can pray with you about your pain? It will help defuse the anger.

_____

_____

_____

_____

_____

Notes

Chapter Ten

CARRY ON!

When I think about moving on, or carrying on, I think about getting on with one's life. Getting from point A to point B. A lot of things hinder us from growing and moving to the next stage. Sometimes it is not knowing when we have reached a plateau. We think we are still growing but we aren't. We allow our contentment to become blockage. Contentment is good, but when we are satisfied with the status quo we are like a stagnant pool without any outlet. The blockage does not allow the pool to drain or receive new water from a different source. The freedom to flow and grow must also be consistent in our lives. We must continue sharing the process with others. We have to carry on.

John 14:
"'Don't be troubled. You trust God, now trust in me. There are many rooms in my Father's home, and I am

going to prepare a place for you. If this were not so, I would tell you plainly. When everything is ready, I will come and get you, so that you will always be with me where I am. And you know where I am going and how to get there.'

'No, we don't know, Lord,' Thomas said. 'We haven't any idea where you are going, so how can we know the way?'

Jesus told him, 'I am the Way, the Truth, and the Life. No one can come to the Father except through me. If you had known who I am, then you would have known who my Father is. From now on you know him and have seen him!'

Philip said, 'Lord, show us the Father and we will be satisfied.'

Jesus replied, 'Philip, don't you even yet know who I am, even after all the time I have been with you? Anyone who has seen me has seen the Father! So why are you asking to see him? Don't you believe that I am in the Father and the Father is in me? The words I say are not my own, but my Father who lives in me does his work through me. Just believe that I am in the Father and the Father is in me. Or at least believe because of what you have seen me do.

The truth is, anyone who believes in me will do the same works I have done, and even greater works, because I am going to be with the Father. You can ask for anything in my name, and I will do it, because the work of the Son brings glory to the Father. Yes, ask anything in my name, and I will do it.

If you love me, obey my commandments. And I will ask the Father and he will give you another Counselor, who will never leave you. He is the Holy Spirit, who leads into all truth. The world at large cannot receive him, because it isn't looking for him and doesn't recognize him. But you do, because he lives with you now and later will be in you. No, I will not abandon you as orphans—I will come to you. In just a little while the world will not see me again, but you will. For I will live again, and you will too. When I am raised to life again, you will know that I am in my Father, and you are in me, and I am in you. Those who obey my commandments are the ones who love me. And because they love me, my Father will love them, and I will love them. And I will reveal myself to each one of them.'

Judas (not Judas Iscariot, but the other disciple with that name) said to him, 'Lord, why are you going to reveal yourself only to us and not to the world at large?'

Jesus replied, 'All those who love me will do what I say. My Father will love them, and we will come to them and live with them. Anyone who doesn't love me will not do what I say. And remember, my words are not my own. This message is from the Father who sent me. I am telling you these things now while I am still with you. But when the Father sends the Counselor as my representative—and by the Counselor I mean the Holy Spirit—he will teach you everything and will remind you of everything I myself have told you.

I am leaving you with a gift—peace of mind and

heart. And the peace I give isn't like the peace the world gives. So don't be troubled or afraid. Remember what I told you, I am going away, but I will come back to you again. If you really love me, you will be very happy for me, because now I can go to the Father, who is greater than I am. I have told you these things before they happen so that you will believe when they do happen.

I don't have much more time to talk to you, because the prince of this world approaches. He has no power over me, but I will do what the Father requires of me, so that the world will know that I love the Father. Come, let's be going.'" *NLT*

Jesus was basically saying to the disciples, Carry On...

Doesn't this passage express what we feel when we are forced to move from one secure place to another? It is difficult to make that choice and it is hard to leave, but if we have had any influence in the lives of others, we want them to continue on in the good things they have learned from us. Jesus wanted his disciples to carry on because it meant the Word had taken root in their hearts and they would now be teaching those truths to others. Jesus knew as they attempted to carry on, they would also experience joy in serving others and they would not be overwhelmed by His leaving them.

Philippians 1:6
"And I am sure that God, who began the good work within you, will continue his work until it is finally finished on that day when Christ Jesus comes back again!" *NLT*

When I go back to places where I have lived, where I have discipled others, it thrills me to see and hear how they are continuing the work of disciple making. It gives me courage to teach others. I know that the Lord is faithful to His Word and His people ,and we all will rejoice in the good things He does in our midst.

I'm Going Away, So.....

He says, Don't worry about it. You will eventually see Me again and you will also come to be with Me at some point. I can only imagine what the disciples must have thought from what the Scriptures tell us. Like this - We are just getting this thing off the drawing board and you are going to do WHAT? Or how about this one, from the words of Thomas, "We haven't any idea where you are going, so how can we know the way?" Can you see the patience Jesus expresses in this portion of Scripture? I would tend to say; I have spent three years with some of you and you still do not get it! You guys are just not with the program. This project has been over-whelming from day one."

When we give of our time and talents, we expect returns. When we invest in anything, we want to know clearly how our investment is going to come back to us. We have expectations, but do we know the final outcome of those expectations? No! It is God's work. We prepare the soil, we water, we plant, but it is God who gives the increase!

Jesus has committed Himself to us. He has given us the Counselor, the Holy Spirit to be with us as a guide. He has not forsaken us. He does not leave us standing all alone. He is our resource for anything that may be headed our way. He is not only on the same page with us, He composed the book.

Carte Blanche!

When we travel today it is made so simple if we carry our **credit cards**. We can buy anything, and do just about anything, if we have the right credit card. Eventually we do pay, but not at that moment. We have the ability to do whatever is necessary to make life happen. Jesus has given us his credit card.

> "The truth is, anyone who believes in me will do the same works I have done, and even greater works, because I am going to be with the Father." *NLT*

We have been given the authority to build the Kingdom. We have been given **Carte Blanche**. Some of the miracles Jesus did were quite amazing. He healed the sick, He fed thousands, He gave sight to the blind. He took time to touch really sick people and He had time for little children.

We have this authority...we have a lifetime to do His work among those with whom we work, live, and go to school every day. What are we doing? Think about it, we are called to do the kind of miracles Jesus did through prayer and our availability, plus who knows what! It's pretty scary if we think too much about it. What specific things might God call us to do? I find it difficult to put door hangers on my neighbors' doors to invite them to a great fun thing for their children that our church is doing at Christmas time. I really want them to come! I really do want to do those great works, but I honestly get scared. A grown woman who is afraid to witness to her neighbors? What kind of Christian lady are you anyway, Edna? Are you for real? Yes, I am but I am just like the disciples, I am a timid weak person.

Why, then, did Jesus entrust us with such a big responsibility if He knew this about us? Could trusting us with so much have been a mistake? No. God knew the failure Peter was facing, when Jesus asked him, "Do you love me, Peter? Then feed my sheep." Jesus knew of Thomas' weakness when he doubted Him. Knowing we are timid, and weak, he still wants us to be "Jesus with skin on" to our children and to others in need of his love.

I am living in a new neighborhood and my neighbors need the love of Christ in their lives. And you know what? So do I. It is hard for us to minister to those who are so close to us. These neighbors have shown me love and acceptance from day one. What can I do but obey him and share his love.

> "Those who obey my commandments are the ones who love me." *NLT*

Those words have been haunting me. I am trying to believe that perfect love casts out fear. When I am afraid to go where I am supposed to go, and be what I am supposed to be then it reflects on the quality of my love relationship with the Savior.

In one of the previous chapters we discussed what **motivates us**. Building the kingdom should be our prime motivator. It is very difficult to share the hope of Christ when we are bound by the fear of man. We know it is exciting and attractive, but it is intimidating as well. As we try to keep our focus on the Lord we get distracted because we have allowed the cares of this world to trap us. We must believe that He is the **main thing**. Jesus is asking us the question, "Do you love me? Then feed my sheep."

We have been given everything we need to complete the task...**to carry on with the work of bringing others into the Kingdom**. Why then is it so hard to invite children to a program at church? We still have a problem with the Lordship of Christ in our lives. It could be a problem of obedience too. So what if I'm sometimes afraid? What if someone comes to the door while I am hanging the invitation on the door? What do I say? Can you honestly imagine me not having any words to speak? See how we get so caught up in the "what if" fears? We miss the blessing of being able to **carry on**. We must recognize that the Holy Spirit wants to motivate us and he also wants to come along side while we are doing His great work.

> "All those who love me will do what I say. My Father will love them, and the Holy Spirit and Jesus will be with us." *NLT*

We keep forgetting this part. It all boils down to settling the question of establishing who we are in Christ. It makes all the difference in our world and for eternity. We have been given **Carte Blanche** with the freedom to do it all, and the Holy Spirit as our constant companion. He is with us and He will control our fears and He will be our courage. I hope you will get out your socks and go forth. Get the socks!

Calling and Equipping

Jesus calls us and He also equips us for the work He has called us to do. He never sends us out to do anything without also coming along with us. He is so faithful. When we are weak, His strength is made perfect. We know that for now. We believe it with all of our hearts. But there are times when we fall prey to doubt. And then we look at our inadequacies and feel insecure.

I stalled for years and years when I considered writing a book. I had a list of excuses. I didn't know enough, I couldn't write, I didn't have anyone to help me with the editing, I didn't have a publisher. All of these things are true. Finally, God just wiped out all of my excuses and I was left with the truth. If

He calls us to do something He will equip us to do it. The neat thing about this whole book is that my son Tim got involved because I needed his expertise. God called him because I needed him to help me complete the task. God fills in the empty blanks and He sends others to help us when we trust Him.

Ephesians 1:15-18
"Ever since I first heard of your strong faith in the Lord Jesus and your love for Christians everywhere, I have never stopped thanking God for you. I pray for you constantly, asking God, the glorious Father of our Lord Jesus Christ, to give you spiritual wisdom and understanding, so that you might grow in your knowledge of God. I pray that your hearts will be flooded with light so that you can understand the wonderful future he has promised to those **he called**. I want you to realize what a rich and glorious inheritance he has given to his people." *NLT*

How would we have felt if we had been the ones receiving this letter from Paul? He has written these very words to us. We don't always think about being flooded with light so we can understand the wonderful future He has promised to us as a result of His call on our lives. We have all been called to carry on the work of God. We have been promised all authority to do His calling.

Ephesians 2:8-10
"God saved you by his special favor when you believed. And you can't take credit for this; it is a gift from God. Salvation is not a reward for the good things we have done, so none of us can boast about it. For we are God's masterpiece. He has created us anew <u>in Christ Jesus, so that we can do the **good things he planned for us long ago**</u>." *NLT*

We can do it. We can do whatever the task may be as we serve Him, because it is the good work that He planned for us long ago.

Job 42:1-2
"I know that you can do all things. No plan of yours, (God), can be thwarted." *NLT*

This concept blows me right out of the water. As part of His plan, when we are afraid, He will provide courage! When we feel alone, He will provide others to come along side. When we lose our sense of direction, He will guide us by way of the Holy Spirit. I love you, Jesus.

Come, Let's Carry On.

The call Jesus gave was not just for disciples. It is to us as well. We are in this together. We need each other. We cannot do it alone. Your spiritual gifts have been given to encourage me and my gifts have been given to encourage you. We are a great team. I like being on the team. I don't exactly know what position I am playing, but if you will give me the game plan, I think I can do it. I know I can do it, because I will be sure to put on my **socks**. See, I really do need those **socks to remind me** of who I am in Christ. It is Christ who is at work in my life and in yours. We need to be reminded of this.

"Greater is he who is in us than the one who is in the world."

"Jesus said, 'I don't have much more time to talk to you, because the prince of this world approaches. He has no power over me, but I will do what the Father requires of me, so that the world will know that I love the Father.'" *NLT*

Get on your **socks and let's go**. Gather up your courage and let's do this work together. I don't know where you are in His plan to build the Kingdom, but I know that each one of us has a part. We are called to serve and work together. Don't fall into the traps and distractions that may be going on around you in your church or community. Don't get involved with petty stuff. Remember to do **the main thing**. Don't try to be so spiritual that you forget how to take a meal to a sick neighbor.

Let's believe together that God is working in all of our lives. Satan really doesn't have any power over us when we commit our way unto the Lord. When we are out there building the Kingdom he is **powerless**. Jesus knows what he is doing. Satan had to ask permission to tempt Job and Peter. They both had real experiences with the prince of this world, but look what happened to their lives. When you have done battle with the enemy, you are then ready to **CARRY ON**. God has given us our marching papers, I can hear the music now.

We must go through the training in order to be ready for the real battle. We are in a major war. The war of our wills, versus the will of God. The struggle of the old nature, versus the new nature.

Claim Your Mountain

One of my favorite people in the Bible is Caleb. This guy is a hero and role model for me. I am sure he wore socks.

Joshua 14:6-14
"A delegation from the tribe of Judah, led by Caleb son of Jephunneh the Kenizzite, came to Joshua at Gilgal. Caleb said to Joshua, 'Remember what the LORD said to Moses, the man of God, about you and

me when we were at Kadesh-barnea. I was forty years old when Moses, the servant of the LORD, sent me from Kadesh-barnea to explore the land of Canaan. I <u>returned and gave from my heart a good report</u>, but my brothers who went with me frightened the people and discouraged them from entering the Promised Land. <u>For my part, I followed the Lord my God Completely</u>.' So that day Moses promised me, 'The land of Canaan on which you were just walking will be your special possession and that of your descendants forever, because you <u>wholeheartedly</u> followed the LORD my God.'

Now, as you can see, the LORD has kept me alive and well as he promised for all these forty-five years since Moses made this promise—even while Israel wandered in the wilderness. Today I am eighty-five years old. I am strong now as I was when Moses sent me on that journey, and <u>I can still travel and fight as well as I could then</u>. So I'm asking you to give me the hill country that the LORD promised me. You will remember that as scouts we found the Anakites living there in great, walled cities. **But if the LORD is with me, I will drive them out of the land, just as the LORD said**.'

So Joshua blessed Caleb son of Jephunneh and gave Hebron to him as an inheritance. Hebron still belongs to the descendants of Caleb son of Jephunneh the Kenizzite because he <u>wholeheartedly followed the LORD, the God of Israel</u>." *NLT*

Caleb claimed his mountain. He found his strength in the Lord. He believed God for his future. He did not faint or grow weary as he waited for the LORD to bring to pass His promise that the land would be his. The Anakites were still in the land, he had to go out and do battle for what God said was his. We have to assume responsibility and we have to go forth and do it, believing God, as we obey.

Commitment to Persevere

God honors those who persist and persevere. He promises to be with us, He promises to equip us and He promises to sustain us in times of need. We need to obey and we need to have a clear view of what our goals are. Here is a call to persevere.

> **II Corinthians 8:9-11**
> "When Paul was dealing with the matter of giving to the poor, he reminded the church at Corinth to <u>finish what they had started. Carry out the project which you proposed over a year ago with enthusiasm</u>." *NLT*

We have spoken about rewards and goals. It is time to do what we must. We are living in times when people need to hear the Gospel, but they also need to see it being lived out before their eyes. We need to renew ourselves to be students of the word. We need to grasp what it means to be salt and light. The salt has to get out of the salt shaker, the light has to be lifted up on a stand, it has to be taken out from under the basket. We must go beyond the pews of our safe environment. We have to be part of what is happening in our world so we can make ourselves available to go with God's plan and purpose. We talked about flexibility earlier in a previous chapter. Now is the time to **carry on**.

> **I Peter 4:10-11**
> "We need to do the work of Christ in the strength that he provides. God has given gifts to each of you

from his great variety of spiritual gifts. Manage them well so that God's generosity can grow through you. Are you called to be a speaker? Then speak as though God himself were speaking through you. Are you called to help others? Do it with all the strength and energy that God supplies. Then God will be given glory in everything through Jesus Christ. All glory and power belong to him forever and ever. Amen." *NLT*

Perseverance requires discipline. We need to be disciplined by the Holy Spirit. We need His control in our lives, not self-control. We need to persevere and jump on in. There is room for all of us. We each can **carry some responsibility for building the Kingdom**.

Encourage others and you will receive courage.

I will never forget the first time I met Dede Kujawa. She was a cute little blonde girl who my son brought home for us to meet. She let me know in no uncertain terms that she didn't want anything to do with my religion. She had her own faith and she was just fine, thank you very much.

This seemed like a rude introduction to someone who was obviously going to be in our lives. Dan was smitten, or should I say, stricken. I knew she was somehow going to be connected to our family. It was evident to us that Dan wanted her around for the long haul.

I liked her because she was spunky and she reminded me of myself. She knew what she knew, and she wasn't about to be influenced or changed from her thinking without a challenge.

She had her goals, and she was determined. She had put herself through college and she was not someone I wanted to cross. I knew I needed to look at her seriously, and pray that God would give me understanding of her heart. If God didn't give me this insight, we were going to clash, big time.

I spent many hours on campus discipling students, the very campus where Dede went to school. I had met many students like Dede who were equally determined and satisfied with their conception of God. But none of them were going to be in our family. So I took special interest in her.

I began to pray for her and for Dan. I prayed that the Lord would, first of all, give me a love for her. I needed Him to love her through me. I didn't have that kind of love on my own. Secondly, I asked the Lord to help me to have something that she wanted. I wanted to serve her in any way I could.

Dan and Dede would come to our house for Sunday dinner after church. Yes, she would go with Dan to church and then they would come to our house for dinner. Once when she joined me in the kitchen I looked at her and politely asked her to make the salad. I put the salad ingredients on the table. She asked me how to make the salad. I knew then that she had a teachable spirit and she wanted to learn more about cooking.

We began **Cooking Class 101**. What fun! I grew to love this sweet, caring, kind girl. She became my friend and she became Dan's wife. I think I began discipling Dede around the kitchen table while we cooked.

We have such a good friendship. I count on her. She has been there for me when no one else cared or bothered as a listening friend. She was with me, singing "Swing Low, Sweet

Chariot" when Bill went home to be with the Lord. She was with me during the worst time of my life. This person whom I thought might be a real problem became a confidante, a prayer partner, a soul mate. We love each other and sometimes, people think she is my daughter. Can you imagine that! Well, we both do have big hair and she wears her socks with me. She has gone with me when I have been asked to share the Gospel. She has loved my son through thick and thin. She is teaching my grandson to pray. She is faithful to pray with him every night. She is my girlfriend!

Does it pay to invest in people? I would say, "YES, BIG TIME!" Whatever it is God is asking you to do...**Carry On!** You have no conception of how your perseverance will pay off.

I have been able to invest in the lives of Diane Haworth, Cindy Forshee, John and Annette Moore, Mary Rose, Shelly Potts, Leanne Anderson, Ed Gracza, Steve Norman, Terry Drake, Dan Houmes, John Varwig, Sue Taussig, Bev Stobie and many others. I have invested in the lives of my sons, Michael, Timothy, and Daniel as well. Yes, it pays to follow Jesus. It pays to **carry on**!

Fran Galbreath invested in my life. She told me when I was 16 years old that I had great potential for the Lord. She believed in me. She taught me about hiding the Word of God in my heart so I would not sin against God. My Mom has prayed me through more situations than I care to mention.

I think I have been a late bloomer, maybe a little like Caleb. I think that I am probably just getting my second wind. I am finally ready to do this thing. I am ready to assume the roll of **Christian, On The Move!** Can you believe I am even ready for another move? It must be God! **I am ready to change**, risk, fail and choose. I am saying to God daily, OK, what's the agenda for the day? *"I'll do it as soon as I find my socks."*

Consider This:

What hinders you from following Christ? The Lord asked Peter if he loved Him and then told Him to feed his sheep. What thoughts do you have when you think of this question that Jesus asked of Peter? Do you know how to love people with God's love? How have you shown compassion to others lately? Have you told God that you will carry on building His Kingdom? Don't quit. Don't give up.

_____

_____

_____

_____

_____